Daniel Ek, MSc, is a registered psychologist with an acceptance and commitment therapy (ACT) focus and works as a lecturer and mindfulness teacher. He is also the co-founder of Friendship Lab, which provides skills training in the art of strengthening relationships.

Pär Flodin, PhD, has a doctorate in cognitive neuroscience at Karolinska Institutet. There he is now an active researcher in psychiatric epidemiology and maps the prevalence and causes of mental illness.

Frida Bern, MSc, is a certified psychologist with a cognitive behavioural therapy (CBT) focus. In her work, she meets many who struggle with loneliness and relationship problems of various kinds, and she finds great meaning in helping people make changes they might not have thought possible.

T0113045

The Power of Friendship:

How to Create, Maintain and Deepen Relationships

Frida Bern MSc, Daniel Ek MSc and
Pär Flodin PhD

ROBINSON

ROBINSON

First published in Sweden in 2021 as *Länge leve vänner* by Natur & Kultur

First published in Great Britain in 2024 by Robinson

1 3 5 7 9 10 8 6 4 2

A CIP catalogue record for this book
is available from the British Library.

ISBN: 978-1-47214-798-1

Typeset in Palatino LT Std by SX Composing DTP, Rayleigh, Essex
Printed and bound in Great Britain by Clays Ltd, Elcograf S.p.A.

Papers used by Robinson are from well-managed forests
and other responsible sources.

MIX
Supporting
responsible forestry
FSC® C104740

Robinson
An imprint of
Little, Brown Book Group
Carmelite House
50 Victoria Embankment
London EC4Y 0DZ

An Hachette UK Company
www.hachette.co.uk

www.littlebrown.co.uk

CONTENTS

LIST OF EXERCISES
R= Reflection exercises, P= Portable tools, C= Connection games

Chapter 8
Others' response when you've exposed your vulnerability (R)
Still eyebrows (C)
See, ask and give (C)
See and be seen (C)
On the lookout for vulnerability (P)

Chapter 9
Get comfortable being uncomfortable (C)
Asking without demanding (R)
Conversational aikido (P)
The brave question (P)
Turing turns (P)
Forgive and be free (R)

Extra exercises in Appendix 1
The lie-detector (C)
The dating game (C)
Search for similarities (C)
Speaker circle (C)
Checking in (C)
I can relate (C)
Thirty-six questions (C)
The hot seat (C)
Your story and my story (C)
Verbalise your feelings (R)

Preface by Bob Hansson

Bob Hansson is a publicly loved poet, author and philosopher in Sweden. With his humour and depth, he has an ability to make the difficult and abstract accessible and entertaining. He often incorporates psychological research in his lectures and has a great interest in positive psychology and things that matter most to us human beings.

One of the largest studies about human happiness began at Harvard in 1938, and is still ongoing. You will read more about this further on in the book, but when George Valliant had been head of the study for forty-five years he was asked: 'What creates a happy life?' Although he had an immense amount of knowledge in the field, his answer was just one single word: 'Love!'

When thinking about love, it's easy to think about the romantic aspect. But most of the loving relationships that you will have throughout your life will not be with someone you are sleeping with (or, for that matter, with someone you once slept with and hope to get another chance with . . .). I would like to claim that most of your loving relationships are those with friends. But if friendship is the most common loving relationship, it is widely neglected in both academic and fictional publishing. Because of this, I am sure I am not the only one who has neglected my friends. So, this is a book that is needed.

May 18th, 2015. My forty-fifth birthday. I was sitting alone on a chair with a screen in my lap. I received thousands of birthday wishes on Facebook, and a few newspapers even considered my birthday to be news. I remember that the sun was shining, but also that I was lonelier than ever before in my life. And I remember that it brought me to a decision that changed my life.

There was a mid-life crisis in the background to this, and I had for some time avoided social interaction and left gatherings early because I 'had to work' (which, between us, actually meant 'watch Netflix'). I was convinced that I was 'over and out'. Too old, too boring – uninteresting in every way. My social self-esteem was low and became even lower since I never mustered the energy to challenge it. Well, almost never. A few weeks earlier, I had been in a good mood and decided to go out. I took a shower and even that felt a little new. 'I got my life back,' I thought, and grabbed my shaving gel. Then, I caught a glimpse of myself in the mirror. Full body. That was enough for my mood to crash down again. Loneliness does something to your gaze, you see – it makes it more harsh. The lonely eye doesn't always create the most compassionate gaze.

I did go out that night, but I returned home pretty quickly. That's a pattern that you may be able to relate to. At times when you need others the most, it's the hardest to be with them.

So, a few weeks after this short night out, I was sitting on a chair and realised that I didn't have a single person who wanted to have cake with me. I had called all the people I felt comfortable with in Malmö. Both were busy. I had become as lonely as I, in younger years, had seen my father become. He used to sit in the woods and really only brightened when speaking of his youth. It was a loneliness that I had never thought that I could fall into, but that was now devouring me. So, I made a decision – to make different choices in the future. Because two things struck me. One was that I am always pregnant with my own future self. The choices I make today create who I become tomorrow. I realised that I spent much less time with my friends now than I did five years ago. I didn't want that trend to continue, because whatever I wanted to give the future version of myself – it surely wasn't more loneliness. The other thing that struck me was that all the research I usually mentioned in my lectures possibly applied even to me.

The Harvard researcher Shawn Achor closely studied new students to find the main theme for success. What did the successful students have in common? He spent a whole year conducting in-depth interviews and then followed up on their accomplishments, and discovered something very astonishing: There was no main theme!

Apparently, it wasn't about intelligence, not about background, not earlier grades, not about if the interviewed students were single or in a relationship. Spending that amount of time only to discover nothing was obviously an academic failure. But, around the same time, Google launched a similar project. They wanted to find out which teams were the most efficient. What did members of successful teams have in common? They continued for years. They studied hundreds of variables in 150 teams all around the world. Google is supposedly the best in the world at analysing data, but they didn't discover a single common denominator.

You see, both Shawn Achor and Google made the same mistake. They searched for individual qualities where they should have searched for relational ones. Google finally concluded that the teams that were the most successful were better at one single thing – creating a good atmosphere in the group. In the end, Shawn at Harvard also discovered something similar – the most successful students were more active and more content with their relationships than the others.

Relationships outrank performance. Consequently, as a careerist, one should not merely make an effort on the job, but amongst one's friends as well. If you have children, you should not only remind them of their homework but, more importantly, to not neglect their friends. At least if you want to be rational.

For me, life has had its ups and downs. That doesn't make me unique in any way. Sometimes life is a walk in the park and sometimes we are tripping over old, dirty laundry. But looking back on my life, the happy periods have neither depended on the level of success, nor on the heat in my romantic relationships. I have been the happiest when I have had good friends – that is, friends that I really like and see often.

In a fascinating experiment, researchers had a number of people stand and look at a long staircase and guess how many steps it consisted of. Most guessed a hundred steps. Then another group of people looked at the same staircase, but they had a friend who was standing some way away. They guessed an average of seventy steps. To me, it's quite incomprehensible that one's view can change so radically just by having a friend nearby. Granted, guessing the number of steps isn't an important skill in modern life, but what if our thoughts about not being able to manage a certain difficulty and therefore going home and watching TV instead, totally changed if we had a friend nearby?

So, what is your life like right now? Are you lonelier than you would like to be? Do you spend as much time as you would like with your friends? Do you spend more or less time with your friends now than you did ten years ago? If your answer is less, it is likely that you will spend even less time with them in another ten years. Is that what you want? If not, I have some good news: The only thing you need to do in order to prevent that is to read this book and do the suggested exercises. These exercises can change your everyday life, and thereby your future. Sure, you can skip them and read the book as some people read cookbooks, with a firm determination to absolutely not cook any food yourself but just read about others doing it. But for me, these exercises really made a difference.

On that chair, nine years ago, I decided to accept every social invitation, even when I didn't feel like it. Jeez, I was pregnant with my future self. My whole future was at stake. Even if I had no desire whatsoever to meet anyone, I would walk out of the door anyway because I was working on my long-term goal: becoming less lonely, becoming more together.

It's easy to say that you don't live to work, but work to live. But how many times have I refrained from working to grab a beer with a friend in comparison to how many times I've cancelled a beer with a friend to work instead?

Furthermore, there is a myth that says that it's harder to make new friends the older you get. A myth both my father and I have used as an excuse for our social laziness. But since I decided to prioritise friends, things started to change faster than I had expected. Just a few weeks after my decision, an acquaintance called and asked if I wanted to come along to a party. That was the starting point of what is now a profound friendship.

One month later, I met Janu for the first time. Today we see each other every week and have started giving classes together. Six months after that I met Henrik for the first time. Today we live together. Janu and Henrik are both pros at being friends and I do my best to mimic them. I do need to practise.

Since I started to prioritise friendships, I have strangely enough quadrupled my income. So perhaps the research isn't completely off-base – even the economy is relative. Updating your friendship situation may be as important in your life as changing jobs or romantic partners, and certainly more important than buying new curtains. The fact that there are more home decor magazines than magazines about friendship is mind baffling.

I wish you luck on your journey with this book and just want to say that every page is worth your time. Reading this book was, to me, an excellent life investment. Because what the heck is the point of friends if you don't prioritise them?

About the authors

The starting point of the friendship between us authors was when Pär found his favourite book on a friend's couch. It turned out to belong to Daniel, who had slept on that couch the night before. Frida came into the picture a few years later, after having met Daniel at the release party of his first book, *The Mindfulness and Acceptance Workbook for Stress Reduction*. One Sunday morning not long after that, Frida received a message from him:

Hi Frida! For a long time, I've been wanting to write a book about friendship, seeing as it's an area that provides joy and meaning in life, and protects us against mental illness and stress. Yet it seems to be an overlooked area – there are few books about its value, how to make friends, strengthen friendships, and so on. I'm looking for a fellow psychologist to write the book with and I thought of you. Would you be interested in talking more about this?

This was the origin of our book *The Power of Friendship*. The authors are two psychologists (Daniel Ek and Frida Bern) and a public health researcher (Pär Flodin). Daniel got the idea of writing this book after a few stressful years of being self-employed as a clinical psychologist and lecturer, working many hours alone. He realised that the main cause of his stress wasn't a heavy workload (because he wasn't all that busy), but the fact that he hadn't prioritised spending time with his friends. Around that time, he also founded 'The Friendship Lab', an initiative to spread knowledge and develop exercises and techniques to deepen relationships.

Pär started his research career as a neuroscientist at the Karolinska Institute. He is currently doing research in the field of psychiatric epidemiology and studies the causes and prevalence of mental disease in the population. A personal motive for writing this book has been his own experiences of enriching friendships, which he has prioritised over many years. For example, in his twenties he 'friendship-married' a close friend to honour their strong (asexual) friendship bond. The ceremony was held under blooming apple trees in front of teary-eyed parents.

For Frida, it has long been crystal clear that social connection is key to her own wellbeing, and that she has been strongly influenced by having such solid friendships throughout her life. Also, as a psychologist, in sessions with her patients, she is often struck by how indispensable close relationships can be for one's wellbeing. The offer of co-authoring this book was well timed. It came when she was feeling quite depressed, having moved over 400 miles away from her friends in order to take a job in another part of the country. At first, the message above made her laugh ('How the heck do you write a book about friendship?'). However, after a moment of doubt about whether or not it would be possible, she felt it was evident that this was something she wanted to try.

Even though the writing of this book paradoxically has meant that we've had to devote our weekends and vacations to writing rather than being with friends and close ones, we are happy that we took on the task. It has been incredibly educational, and above all it has helped us value our friendships even more. We hope to inspire you to do the same.

INTRODUCTION
Why friendship?

How many dull conversations have we had around the coffee machine? How many opportunities have we missed as we let our phones steal attention away from the friend we are with? What if we had been better at showing how important we really were to one another? What if we had been taught as children that one of the greatest impacts on how long and well we live is the extent to which we take care of our friendships? What would our lives have been like then?

Friendship – a matter of health

It was in the beginning of 2018 that we authors began to seriously consider questions such as: Why do we so often let friendships fall by the wayside when making important, life-altering decisions about where to live and work? Why do we neglect our friendships as the demands of work, romantic relationships and family life increase? Despite all the growth and joy our friends gave us, we didn't prioritise them as much as we would have liked. As we looked around, many others seemed to be doing the same. How did this happen?

Although friendships are one of the most important aspects of life, we grow up without any formal training in how to nurture them. In primary school, we learned the names of rivers and medieval kings, but nothing about the health aspects of friendship. If there is any education offered in how to establish and maintain close relationships, it almost always refers to romantic ones. Education about love and sex is all well and good, but as traditional couple relationships become more fluid (fewer marry and more divorce than ever before), our lasting friendships become increasingly important.

The theme of friendship is also widely lacking in self-help books. In libraries and bookshops, there are as many books about love as there are about food. Yet there is barely more written about *how to nurture your friendships* than there is about *how to take care of your toothbrush*. In addition, our society clearly doesn't support our friendships to the same extent as it does our family groupings and love lives. For example, legal institutions and regulations about mortgages and home insurance pay very little regard to friendship. We are inundated with (more or less direct) messages about the importance of getting a job, a family, and material abundance, yet it is surprisingly rare that we are ever encouraged to prioritise friendship. On the contrary, we are encouraged to move to cities that can offer jobs and education, leaving behind our social networks. Why so? We authors have only been able to speculate about this question, but we agree on the following: Given how valuable friendship is, it deserves more attention and a higher status than we tend to give it.

Social contact is increasingly considered to be a public health issue. As medical science has become better at treating and curing diseases, there has been an increased understanding of how environmental and social factors contribute to their origin. We now know that, for many of our common diseases, the *social* environment is as critical as the *physical* – like the air we breathe and the food we eat. The negative health effects of loneliness have been increasingly noticed – something that led to the UK being the first country in the world to appoint a political minister with a responsibility to lead on reducing loneliness.

Efforts to counteract loneliness are needed for people of all ages and, when put into play early, they reduce the risk of loneliness in the elderly. 'Habits formed at an early age give long-term results – effects that we often don't notice until we are older,' says Julianne Holt-Lunstad, professor of psychology at Brigham Young University. We will discuss her research further in Chapter 1. She wishes to see more *preventive* measures and has, among other things, suggested specific guidelines for social contact, similar to our guidelines for diet, exercise and sleep. Lisa Berkman, professor of epidemiology at the University of California, who in 1979 published the first solid evidence of the connection between social relationships and health, shares this opinion. She advises us to contemplate what we can do *as early in life as possible*, as that can help us create and maintain the type of relationships we want and can benefit from in the long run. We authors agree and our ambition with this book is to help you do just that.

An impossible and urgent project

While writing, we've had a recurring feeling that we've taken on an almost impossible task. To write a handbook on how to deepen friendship is no less pretentious than writing a manual on how to live a good life. Do we suffer from hubris? Who do we think we are? Admittedly, all three of us enjoy close friendships (and we are truly thankful for and proud of the social lives that we have been lucky enough to establish), but we can hardly give ourselves the title of friendship experts (especially not before we started writing this book). Just like many others, we have neglected our friendships while entering new romantic relationships, only to feel lonely and confused when they have ended. Throughout the years, we have struggled with illnesses, self-improvement projects and endless to-do lists. One of the most important sources that we have repeatedly come back to in order to replenish our energy has been our friends. Nevertheless, we have of course faced the same difficulties as anyone else, and we don't have any miracle cures to get rid of them.

There are, however, a lot of experts in relationship psychology, whose valuable knowledge and experience don't always reach the general public. There are strategies that are more helpful than others. Our ambition has been to map out and introduce them, so that they can hopefully be of help to you and many others.

Content and layout

The first two chapters of the book are the most theoretical. In the very first, we discuss how indispensable people are to each other, and go through a few studies that describe the connection between good social relationships and mental and physical health. In Chapter 2, we dive deep into the nature of friendship and focus on the characteristics of close friendships. If you are already eager to get started with the exercises and contact-promoting skills, you can go straight to Chapter 3 and continue on from there.

In Chapter 3, we guide you to reflect on your friendships: What is your current situation, how would you like it to be, and what would you like to develop? There are also useful tips and inspiration for those who wish to find new friends or find it hard to make room for social interaction in everyday life. The following chapter is about how good friendships can be made or deepened. Many of the methods described in the book may initially feel a little unusual and formal. Changing social habits and developing new relational skills are often life-long processes of 'trial and error'. So be patient and lenient with yourself! Just like practising other skills, it takes commitment, and you will need to try and test the new. The more dedicated you are, the more you will benefit from this book. Our advice is therefore to really practise the methods and explore the exercises as much as you can.

The exercises come in three different categories: *Reflection exercises, connection games*, and *portable tools*. The *reflection exercises* can mostly be done on your own and often require some kind of writing tool. *Connection games* are done with one or several friends. The *portable tools* are keys to use 'in the field', in the interactions of your everyday life. It can be beneficial to read the book together with a friend. Why not offer it as a gift to a friend you wish to deepen your relationship with?

This book focuses on friendships between *adults*, and how these relationships may be deepened by being truly present in meetings. Of course, the feeling of warmth, security and friendship can emerge in many different ways and with more beings than just other adults. For instance, we can feel a strong sense of connection when we roll around on the floor with our dog, cuddle with a small child, or even when we look at that ancient tree outside our bedroom window. Without diminishing your relationship with your dog or the neighbour's playful toddler, we have chosen to limit this book to friendships between adults. A topic that is certainly broad enough.

Theoretical pillars

The book is largely based on modern psychology and especially on methods within the framework of behavioural therapy. One of these is *acceptance and commitment therapy*, or ACT. An important part of ACT is increasing our *psychological flexibility*. It is strengthened when we develop different approaches that help us see our thoughts and feelings for what they are (conceptions and changeable conditions, rather than absolute truths) and *simultaneously* move us towards what we value as important in our lives. The opposite is *psychological rigidity*, which is when we get stuck in judgemental thoughts about ourselves or others, hold on to strategies that don't work, and do things that feel good in the moment but that, long term, lead us away from the life that we wish to lead. Studies show that the greater our psychological flexibility is, the higher we rate our quality of life.

The field of therapy that has inspired us the most is *functional analytic psychotherapy*, or FAP. This method was founded in the 1990s by the psychologists Mavis Tsai and Robert Kohlenberg, who wanted to seize the healing power of authentic, interpersonal interactions. Their colleague Jonathan Kanter is head of the Center for the Science of Social Connection (CSSC) at the University of Washington. His research, compiled articles and books within the field are a great source of inspiration for us. We have also been very inspired by Mavis Tsai's later initiative that she calls ACL-groups. The acronym ACL stands for *awareness, courage* and *love*, and many professionals within the field of FAP use these three words to summarise behaviours that seem to be crucial for creating close bonds. In Chapter 2, you will find an initial introduction to the science behind these concepts.

Many of the models, exercises and games in this book come from the movement *authentic relating*. It emerged at the end of the 1990s in San Francisco and gathered together people who wanted to create more meaningful and authentic encounters and relationships. The movement has grown steadily and spread to several continents. There is no pivotal person or organisation; instead, the games and exercises are co-created and continuously developed by the users.

Lastly, we have gathered inspiration from the conflict management method *non-violent communication* (NVC, also referred to as the giraffe language, after the giraffe who has the biggest heart of all land-living animals). The founder of NVC is Marshall Rosenberg, psychologist and conflict mediator, who in the early 1960s started teaching the conversation method to reduce conflict and create more peace and understanding in relationships and in society. Courses and longer educational programmes are now available to the general public in many countries, and many books have been written on the subject. If you are interested in learning more about NVC there is a lot of free material available online.[1]

New strategies – not new rules

An important starting point for both ACT and FAP is that everything that we humans do, all our behaviours, meet some kind of need and are a consequence of our earlier learning. Both methods also emphasise the significance of the context. Just like a single word in this book wouldn't mean anything to you if it were torn from its context, our behaviours need a context to be understandable and meaningful.

Many books give a somewhat simplified view of people, for instance by categorising us into different personality colours or advocating rules like 'Be honest!' Simple explanations such as these have a strong attractive force on us, since reality, especially when it comes to relationships, is so dynamic and complex. However, there are several

---

1 For example, the founder of NVC, Marshall Rosenberg, has a three-hour-long introductory lecture on YouTube. It's called 'NVC Marshall Rosenberg – San Francisco Workshop'.

risks with this, for example that we cultivate psychological rigidity rather than flexibility. Someone who reads a book that advocates being honest may start to blurt out all their 'truths' to their partner and their boss, without a delicate awareness of the context in which they follow this advice. We would rather strengthen your ability to be flexible and adjust your strategies in accordance with what's happening here and now.

Although we in this book express how connection can be deepened, we want to make it clear that the exercises and advice must be valued in relation to their actual results in different situations. For example, what would be the result of you honestly expressing your feelings as opposed to politely discussing something that feels tediously boring? With that said, it's time for the first chapter: *A matter of life and death.*

CHAPTER 1
A matter of life and death

Our time on this Earth is limited and we never know when it's going to end. Are you living your life as you would like? Take a minute to think about the following:

If you continue living your life just as you are doing now, what could you wish to have done differently upon facing your death?

It's a big question and it can stir up emotions. Perhaps you want to rush forward. We suggest you see what happens if you don't do that, but instead stop and contemplate.

So, did you think of something that feels genuine to you? Maybe you would wish that you had spent less time working and more time pursuing a passion in life? Or that you had spent more time with your family and friends? Not having prioritised relationships was one of the most common regrets of people on their deathbeds, according to an article from 2009 that was widely spread on the internet and then became a book titled *The Top Five Regrets of the Dying*. It was written by the Australian nurse Bronnie Ware, who cared for and interviewed hundreds of people in their final stages of life. She found that many didn't realise until their last few weeks, when it was too late, that they had let valuable friendships slip through their fingers.

Many of us take for granted that friends are important and good. When we asked around in our communities about *why*, we received many different answers:

- Friends provide a sense of meaning and context.
- A close friend can listen and support you.
- With close friends you can be yourself and don't need to perform.
- Friends can help you move to a new flat, babysit and other practical stuff.
- You can have *fun* with friends – just laugh, goof around and let loose.
- A network of friends can help you with contacts that open up new opportunities.
- Friends broaden your horizons, give you new perspectives and break up your regular thought patterns.
- Life is less predictable with friends.
- Close friends can give you honest answers and see through your bullshit.
- You feel less lonely with friends.

One might say there is no need for scientific evidence to prove that friends both facilitate and enrich our lives. But as a matter of fact, there is an abundance of studies that both confirm our intuition, and go further. In this chapter, we will go through an overview of the compiled research that proves that friends are more than just *good*, friends are *vital*!

Do friends make us happier?

Daniel Kahneman is a psychologist and researcher in decision making, and plays a pivotal role in the field of behavioural economics. Perhaps he is most well known for his book *Thinking, Fast and Slow*. In a study from 2004, he asked what makes us the happiest in our daily lives, and found that the majority of the almost one thousand working women who participated in the study were happiest while spending time with their near and dear ones. They felt the least happy while working or commuting to or from work.

Kahneman's study design was simple. He asked the participants to describe what they had done and experienced the day before – how much time they had spent doing various activities, and what emotions they experienced while doing them. A justified objection to this method is that people tend to have a somewhat distorted memory of what actually made them happy in a particular moment. In order to circumvent that, the psychology researcher Mihaly Csikszentmihalyi (the man who came up with the concept of *flow* – the sense of complete presence that can be experienced while being completely absorbed by an activity) let the participants of his study report their experiences in *real time*. He and his colleagues equipped eight hundred grade school students with a wristwatch that randomly throughout the day asked them, then and there, to report their emotional state and what they were doing. The results were published in 2003 and, hardly surprisingly, the authors reported a similar conclusion as Kahneman – socialising with friends was by far the strongest variable for happiness. Eating food and watching TV were much less auspicious and the students were the least happy while doing their homework.

That we are happy while spending time with friends may sound obvious, but what roles do friends and friendships play when it comes to our long-term wellbeing? One way to approach this question is to investigate how the happiest people live their lives. In the study 'Very happy people' from 2002, Martin Seligman, a foreground figure in the research field of positive psychology, interviewed two hundred students and found that what distinguished the happiest ones was that they had particularly satisfactory relationships. They also spent more time with other people in general.

OUR FRIENDS' FRIENDS' FRIENDS AFFECT US

In 2009 an acclaimed book, *Connected*, was published, compiling research on how we are affected by our social networks. The authors, Nicholas Christakis, professor of sociology at Harvard, and James Fowler, professor of medical genetics at the University of California, presented evidence that our friends' friends' friends – people we have never met and that we don't share a single strand of DNA with – have a surprisingly high impact on our lives. Several of the studies they referred to are based on the Framingham Heart Study, where thousands of people in the city of Framingham, Massachusetts, have been monitored since 1948, with data collected about their physical and mental wellbeing.

One of the discoveries was that overweight people had more over-weight people in their networks than others, even though they weren't related or even knew about each other. Consequently, the phenomenon couldn't quite be explained by them sharing a hereditary predisposition or by them being directly influenced by each other's diets and exercise habits. Neither could the findings be explained by their socioeconomic status. When overweight people died, new people who were also over-weight joined the networks. Christakis describes it as the networks living their own lives and having their own structures.

In another analysis, the researchers wanted to study whether or not 'happiness' could spread throughout social networks in a similar way, and it surely could. When a 'happy' person (according to the scale used in the study), came into someone else's network, the chances of the latter person reporting happiness increased. Christakis refers to this as 'network transmission' and claims that we are affected by people as far as three steps away from us, even though we've never even met them. The 'network transmission' applies to a wide variety of things, ranging from how happy we are, to how much weight we gain and lose, and to how we make love. If a person in our network, three steps away from us, starts going to the gym, the probability increases that we too will start going to the gym. Hence you can say that our friends and our friends' friends and our friends' friends' friends contribute to shaping who we are – we are interconnected.

Do friends make us healthier?

In the comprehensive 'Harvard study of adult development', research-ers have followed hundreds of men in the Boston area since the 1930s. The study is still ongoing and is one of the longest conducted studies ever performed. From all the collected data (brain scans, blood sam-ples, questionnaires, and interviews with the men and those close to them), the researchers have been able to conclude that close relation-ships seem to affect our physical wellbeing *more* than wealth, levels of cholesterol, work or social status. In 2015, the head of the research study, Robert Waldinger, summed up the results in a TEDx-talk: 'When we took a look at everything we knew about the men when they were around fifty years old, it wasn't their cholesterol levels that predicted how they would age – it was how satisfied they were in their relationships. The men that were the happiest in their relationships in their fifties were those who were the healthiest when they were eighty.'

Several other studies point in the same direction. The Canadian author and psychologist Susan Pinker has, in her book *The Village Effect*, summarised research about what causes residents in some regions to live much longer than residents in similar neighbouring regions. She reports that what matters is both the number of people that you interact with and *how close* your relationships with them are. These close relationships refer to relationships characterised by a high level of trust. How do you measure that? For example, the answer to the question 'How many people do you feel comfortable asking to help you move?' can reflect the extent to which you surround yourself with people you trust. Pinker states that the more confiding relationships people have, and the more people they interact with in everyday life, the higher the probability that they will live a long life.

Correspondingly, there is extensive research that proves it can be truly harmful for your body and health to be socially isolated. Psychology professor Julianne Holt-Lunstad (whom we wrote about in the introduction) published a large overview study in 2015, that illustrates the connection between premature death, experienced loneliness and social isolation. Based on a compilation of seventy different scientific studies with data from 3.4 million people around the world, she concluded that those who consider themselves lonely or those who are socially isolated have a 30 per cent higher risk of dying during a given period of time.

When speaking of social isolation, researchers refer to a person having fewer social relationships compared to other people in the surrounding area. Experienced loneliness, on the other hand, refers to the difference between the *desired* number of close relationships and the *actual* amount. The authors of the article concluded that both are equally important – the experience of loneliness, but also actually having few relationships. Each of these factors on their own affects the risk of premature death to the same extent as other well-known risk factors, such as being overweight and smoking. Loneliness reduces a person's lifespan as much as alcoholism or smoking fifteen cigarettes per day, according to Holt-Lunstad.

Which is the chicken and which is the egg?

There is a clear *connection* between close social relationships and a longer and healthier life. But how can we be sure that it is the close relationships that are keeping people healthy? Wouldn't it also be possible that good health and wellbeing facilitate the development and maintenance of close relationships? And that people who, for one reason or another, already have poor physical or emotional health have a higher risk of becoming lonely and isolated?

In order to avoid jumping to faulty conclusions like the typical example of 'high ice cream sales *cause* sunshine' (based on the observation that more people buy ice cream when it's sunny), more is needed than an *association connection*. By monitoring people over time and keeping all other factors (that could possibly affect the studied phenomenon) constant, you can, however, draw more well-grounded conclusions about whether or not a change (such as increased or decreased social contact) *causes* another (improved or deteriorated health). If people *first* increase their number of social contacts and *then* become healthier, it indicates that social contact causes positive health effects.

Someone whose research results support that loneliness can *precede* the development of symptoms of depression was John T. Cacioppo, professor of social neuroscience at the University of Chicago. Together with his colleague Louise C. Hawkley, he monitored 229 middle-aged people over a period of five years. Each year, the participants were put through a series of tests and filled out various self-assessment questionnaires, for example the *UCLA Loneliness Scale*. Furthermore, the researchers conducted extensive interviews to map out the participants' social networks. This study plan with repeated tests allowed the researchers to see that when someone became less lonely, their symptoms of depression also decreased.

It has long been known that there is a connection between social isolation and risk for dementia, but it has yet to be ruled out that it isn't the cognitive impairments that lead to less socialising rather than the other way around. However, in a study from University College, London, published in 2019, researchers found evidence to support that social isolation can contribute to the *origin* of the disease. They followed ten thousand participants and collected data over a period of twenty-eight years, adjusting for (that is, ruling out that the connection could be explained by) other relevant factors such as education, employment and socioeconomic status. The study showed that participants who at sixty years of age had almost daily contact with friends, had significantly lower risk of developing dementia later in life.

In research, there is an expression that 'one study is no study', to remind us not to jump to conclusions based on the results of a few, smaller studies. Instead, reviewing the compiled research within a field leads to a more reliable conclusion. In an overview study like this, psychology researcher Joyce Siette and her colleagues compiled fourteen large studies that all assessed the health effects of letting elderly people and people with mental health issues spend time with volunteers. In all, these studies included up to 2,500 participants. The typical set-up was that the participants met with a volunteer for about one hour every week over a period of three months, in order to receive social support – a kind of temporary friendship. Siette and her colleagues reported that, despite the low number of meetings and hours with the volunteers, the participants experienced significant health improvements. The study especially shows that affirmative relationships, being with somebody who cares, can actually *cause* better health.

Dependent on connection

In the psychologist John B. Watson's bestselling book, *Psychological Care of Infant and Child*, from 1928, he wrote that too much love and cuddles from parents could cause irreversible damage to children. Today we have a radically changed approach, and someone who has contributed a lot to that is the psychology researcher Harry Harlow. In the 1940s, he started to conduct controversial experiments on rhesus monkeys. In some of his more brutal experiments, baby monkeys were locked into isolation cells called 'the Cage of despair'. Sadly enough, they could be kept locked up for up to two years without any form of contact with other beings. Today, few people would be surprised to hear that these monkeys developed serious behavioural disturbances.

Harlow's experiments were cruel, but they contributed to people's understanding that our basic needs consist of more than just food and sleep. Nowadays, newborn babies are not separated from their parents, but are instead held very close, preferably skin-to-skin.

Since we have always lived in, and to a large extent *survived* thanks to, our social groups, it has been important for us to keep track of people – who can we depend on in hardships and who can we relax with during calmer times? We have always been dependent on contact with others, and with that in mind it's probably not a coincidence that loneliness can be so painful. Just as we can get a stomach ache when we are hungry and need food, the pain of loneliness can be interpreted as a signal that we have a need for connection. Ideally, it will motivate us to seek contact, establish new relationships or nurture the ones we already have.

Researchers are continuously finding more evidence to support that these phenomena aren't uniquely human. Friendship, or something that resembles friendship (they have not yet agreed on what to call it), has been identified in a surprisingly large number of species. The anthropologist Joan Silk's work shows that female baboons form friendship-like relationships, and that those who have them don't just live longer themselves – their offspring also have a higher chance of surviving. These results have been replicated and other researchers have been able to prove that they apply not only to baboons, chimpanzees and primates, but also to other mammals such as elephants, hyenas, whales and dolphins. Even animals as simple as zebrafish demonstrate interesting social behaviours. When they can smell their 'friends', they exhibit less of the stress-behaviour to freeze (or 'play dead'). If they also can *see* their friends, their stress is reduced even more.

These findings suggest that we humans are not alone when it comes to finding loneliness difficult. That we, as well as other animals, suffer pain and become stressed out by social isolation can be understood in the light of the fact that we have been dependent on social connection for thousands of years. It seems to be deeply rooted in our biology.

QUALITY AND QUANTITY

In the early 1970s, Mark Granovetter, a sociologist at Stanford University, presented an idea that became significantly influential. In the article 'The strength of weak ties', he accounted for how weak ties to others can entail a certain strength. Having a network of acquaintances can facilitate your life. For example, it can make it easier for you to find a new job or a new place to live, and get greater access to new information and knowledge. Conversely, the lack of such a network can cause difficulties, when you only have a few people to refer to (if you have ever moved to a new town or emigrated to a new country, you can probably relate to this). At the same time, research indicates that strong, stable and supporting relationships entail particular health advantages, both in humans and in other species.

When researchers have studied how monkeys' social relationships affect their resilience against SIV (the monkey equivalent of HIV), they found that the monkeys do better if they continue to see the *same* monkeys compared to if they see *new* monkeys every day. All of the monkeys in this experiment had equal opportunities to socialise with others, but the virus developed more rapidly in the group that was deprived of the opportunity to form stable relationships.

When the anthropologist Joan Silk (whose research we referred to earlier) and her research team studied more closely what kind of social relationships contribute to some female baboons living longer and even having more surviving offspring, the main factor proved to be *strong* and *stable* relationships with other female baboons (it even seemed to be enough with just three such relationships to obtain the effect).

Another researcher who has shown an interest in how the *quality* of our relationships affects our health is the social psychologist Bert Uchino, at the University of Utah. He has concluded that bad relationships can be linked to higher levels of symptoms of depression, higher blood pressure and a weakened immune system. Close relationships, however, are linked to less cardiovascular problems and fewer biological markers of ageing. Just like Holt-Lunstad and Waldinger, Uchino concludes it is the actual experience of having close, supportive relationships which has the biggest impact on our health.

The biological link between friendship and health

Most would agree that hormones and neurotransmitters are involved in the relationship between parent and child (during pregnancy, childbirth, breastfeeding, etc.). Likewise, the significance of our biology seems obvious in sexual relationships. However, it is not as evident that non-sexual friendship relations also affect our bodies. Perhaps that is why the connection between physical health and social support mainly has been practically explained, for example 'If you are alone you don't have anyone to drive you to the hospital and no one to help you understand that you need to go there.' However, that doesn't seem to be the *whole* explanation – social connection impacts us in more ways and on deeper levels than that.

To try to understand why some population groups in the USA recovered better than others from breast cancer, researchers (Gretchen Hermes at Yale School of Medicine, and others) chose to study rats – a social animal that is biologically pretty similar to a human. In one study, female rats were divided into two groups – half of them were isolated in their own cages and the other half got to live with family and friends. The researchers found that the isolated rats became less curious about their surroundings. They also secreted ten times the amount of stress hormones when they were exposed to stress. But the most interesting discovery was that the isolated rats developed significantly more *and* bigger tumours in their mammary glands, and that these tumours were to a higher degree malignant.

Loneliness and inflammation

When we feel lonely or risk being rejected or expelled from our group we become stressed. The brain signals to the rest of the body that we are facing a threat and the body replies by activating its stress system, that is to say the sympathetic nervous system (see below). A cascade of hormones and physiological processes kick in to mobilise the body's resources so that we can fix the problem, eliminate the danger (loneliness), and seek out other people. One of these activated processes is that the immune system prepares to fight possible attackers (bacteria and virus). More white blood cells are made, which temporarily strengthens the immune system and increases the level of inflammation in the body.

If we are involuntarily lonely and thereby stressed for longer periods of time, our immune system becomes less sensitive to the stress hormone cortisol. What cortisol otherwise does is keep the inflammation at a moderate level by 'talking' to the white blood cells. During prolonged stress, the blood cells have trouble understanding the cortisol's message, which results in an increased level of inflammation and difficulty for the body to restore balance.

THE PARASYMPATHETIC AND SYMPATHETIC NERVOUS SYSTEM

The part of the nervous system that we cannot voluntarily control is called the autonomic nervous system. It can be divided into two parts. One is the *sympathetic nervous system*, which is activated when we are exposed to danger or believe we are being threatened in some way. Our so-called fight, flight or freeze response is then activated. Several stress hormones, such as cortisol and adrenaline, are released into the bloodstream, allowing energy to reach our muscles. All of this prepares us to handle the threat. Short term, this strengthens our body and makes us less vulnerable. However, a high level of stress over a prolonged period of time (such as that caused by involuntary loneliness) constantly activates the sympathetic nervous system, causing negative health effects. These include impaired sleep, weakened immune system and indigestion.

The other part, the parasympathetic nervous system, sometimes referred to as the quiet rest and digest system, is activated when we feel safe and secure. It stimulates rest and digestion, builds our body, strengthens our immune system, and helps us recover from stress and challenges. We feel our best when the parasympathetic and the sympathetic nervous systems are alternately activated and there is a balance between the two. This happens when we are exposed to a moderate degree of challenges followed by adequate recovery.

The balancing effect of connection

One of the many things which happen in our bodies when we surround ourselves with people we like and trust is that *oxytocin* is released. It is known as 'the love hormone' and has long been associated with physical touch and breastfeeding, but now there is research to support that oxytocin is also released when we experience social warmth. Oxytocin lowers our blood pressure, moderates the stress hormone cortisol, and reduces activity in the parts of our brains that are activated when we are afraid. Furthermore, oxytocin makes us more inclined to orient towards other people and recognise their smiles and friendly glances. All of this increases the activation of the *parasympathetic nervous system*.

The parasympathetic nervous system includes the *vagus nerve*, also referred to as 'the wandering nerve', since its eighty thousand nerve fibres spread out like a tree with roots and branches in all directions. From the brain stem, it passes through the neck towards the face, ears and eyes, to then pass on to the bowels and most of the larger internal organs. The vagus nerve provides the brain with information about how we feel, but it also plays a role in regulating important functions in the body. It affects our heart rhythm and digestion, but also essential functions to social interaction and communication – the vocal cords, facial and neck muscles, hearing and eye movement.

The vagus nerve's impact on our social relationships has, over the last two decades, triggered an increasing interest from medical professionals and researchers. The American psychologist Barbara Fredrickson describes in her book *Love 2.0* how people with an increased base-level activity in their vagus nerve (a stronger 'vagus tone') are more flexible, both socially and mentally. They more easily adapt to changes and regulate their attention and their emotions. In social contexts, they also have a head start when it comes to establishing positive connections. Not only do people with a strong vagus tone seem to have an easier time establishing positive connections, but positive meetings with others can additionally strengthen the vagus tone. This is most likely one of the reasons that social interaction strengthens our health. The vagus nerve has a calming effect on inflammation. Therefore, by stimulating the vagus nerve, for example by social interactions, it seems possible to lower the degree of inflammation and thereby improve health.

In summary

What if we were to actually apply what so many have sensed and what is now also confirmed by research – that close relationships make us both happier and healthier? Wouldn't 'seeing my friends' be prioritised on our to-do lists? The size of our social networks matters, but it is particularly the quality of our relationships that is significant for our mental and physical health. Therefore, friendship deserves to be ranked higher in communities, health care and in our everyday lives.

In the next chapter, we will explore what characterises strong friendship, what distinguishes close connection and, above all, how to establish and deepen friendships.

CHAPTER 2
A formula for friendship

It's Friday afternoon and you're getting off the crowded bus at the stop near your close friend. You're getting together to cook dinner and you're looking forward to an evening of good conversation and laughter. Your friend opens the door and you enter, take a deep breath and exhale with a sigh, feeling the stress of the week leave your body. Your shoulders are lowered and you feel a sense of relief when crossing your friend's doorstep. There's no need to keep up a facade, be smart or good-looking. You feel safe and comfortable. You feel at home.

For a lot of people, friendship is an ordinary phenomenon – so ordinary that we rarely reflect on what it is. Nevertheless, that's precisely what we are going to do in this chapter. Before you continue reading, we advise you to take a minute to contemplate the following:

If you have, or ever had, a particularly close and supportive friendship – what is, or were, the characteristics of that friendship?

At the end of the 1970s, psychology researcher Mary Parlee at the Massachusetts Institute of Technology compiled the results of a large survey. Almost forty thousand readers of the American magazine *Psychology Today* had answered questions about what qualities they look for in their close friendships and what expectations they have of their friends. The most common answers were:

Trust	*Intimacy*
Honesty	*Warmth*
Acceptance	*Affection*
Loyalty	*Support*

These words indicate that we, with our friends, want to be able to relax and feel comfortable, safe and accepted. If we *can't* do this, we are most likely less inclined to call someone a friend, and maybe even less so a *good* friend. On the other hand, if our view of friendship is too narrow and idealised, we risk missing out on meaningful relationships.

True friendship – is there such a thing?

Aristotle (an ancient Greek philosopher reputed for his classifications) made a point of separating 'true' friendship from friendship that was more based on pleasure than on utility. In movies, such as *Lord of the Rings*, friendship is portrayed as a power strong enough to make Samwise Gamgee willing to sacrifice his life for Frodo. As soon as he hears that Frodo is embarking on a life-threatening journey into the land of the enemy, Mordor, he decides to come with him to support him, no matter what happens.

When we posed the question 'What is friendship?' on social media, a few of the answers we received were: 'A true friend supports you the most when you deserve it the least', 'True friendship is unpretentious, unconditional and timeless', and 'A true friend understands even without the need for words.' But is a true friend someone who is *always* there for you and *never* lets you down, not even when you've had a really bad year, stolen your friend's business idea, or been lousy at keeping in touch? Do you have such an 'always available' person in your network of friends? That may be, but we have also understood that there is an idea of *true* friendship as an almost unattainable ideal.

The longing for friendship that feels genuine and true shouldn't be trivialised. At the same time, such black or white ideas can be problematic, and even give us the impression that friendship is like a destination that we may one day reach, to then settle down. In reality, aren't there endless ways of being friends? Friendships can also often change forms. For example, the degree of closeness tends to vary over time without becoming problematic. Maybe you have sometimes been excited about meeting a friend that you haven't seen in ages. Or heard old friends say things such as 'Whenever we see each other, it feels as if time has stood still and we just pick up where we left off'? A romantic relationship, on the other hand, would most likely have ended pretty quickly if your contact ceased.

In order to not add to the unrealistic and obstructive ideas about friendship, we have chosen to proceed from a metaphor that is a little more flexible than, for example, a list of criteria of what would constitute the 'real deal'. We compare friendship to *strings of pearls of connection*.

Friendship is like a string of pearls of connection

Every now and then, a feeling of a deeper connection can spark between people, for example when you and the person sitting next to you on the bus both smile at the cute child in the seat in front of you. Or when a kind stranger helps you with your heavy suitcase and you stop for a second to make eye contact. It can also occur in moments shared with people you are close to, like when you are completely present with a child, or when your partner holds your hand. When we establish this kind of connection it can feel as if we are 'vibrating' together. Sometimes we say that 'we click', or, if we spend more time together, that we 'have chemistry'. According to Barbara Fredrickson, professor of psychology at the University of North Carolina, these words seem to describe what actually happens in such meetings. Her research has shown that three things occur: we *share positive emotions*, we *feel that we want what's best for one another*, and we *synchronise our behaviours and our bodies*. The latter involves a more or less unconscious coordination of movements, tones of voice and speaking pace, but also involuntary processes, such as heart rhythm and hormone levels.

Even though what we have described above can be seen as important ingredients, friendships obviously include more than just fragments of random moments of deeper connection. Just because you have 'clicked' one time with a person at an event, doesn't mean that you have become friends (even if there is potential). Friendship is developed over time and needs some kind of continuity. With our friends, we collect mutual experiences and memories. We can have internal jokes and jargon that is completely incomprehensible to others. Or close friends have often learned what we need to hear when we're sad and what we *don't* need to hear when we're pouting and moping. Something makes us want to see each other time and time again, and when we get together we don't start over from scratch each time, because we know somewhat where we stand. Friendship can therefore be compared to a string of pearls. The *pearls* are the moments of connection and the *string* is the experience of a lasting relationship.

What strengthens the strings?

The psychology professor Debra Oswald at Marquette University wanted to find out what makes friendships last over time. She let six hundred students answer a large number of questions about how often they did different things with their friends. She also explored whether the behaviours differed depending on how close the friends were. In her compilation from 2004, she concluded that the most distinguishing element of the *close friends* was *positivity* – for example, that they expressed gratitude, made each other laugh and did fun things together. Other significant behavioural categories were *support*, *openness* and *spending time together*. Similar characteristics of friendship have been reported by other researchers, even if some variations occur. For example, the Canadian psychology professor Beverley Fehr states in her book *Friendship Processes* that the most important keys for maintaining friendship are to be *open*, to offer *support* and *acknowledgement*, and to spend *time* together. She also emphasises the importance of *reciprocity*. Daniel J. Canary, researcher of communications at Pennsylvania State University, adds that *laughter* and *humour* are also significant factors.

Coming from our view of friendship as a *string of pearls of connection*, we will now begin by considering what can strengthen the *string* (that makes the friendship last over time). We will then introduce what thirty years of relationship research has to say about how we together create the pearls – the moments of close connection.

Time together

'The exposure effect' is a well-known concept, widely used in marketing contexts. It says that the more we see a product, the more we like it (provided that we begin with a positive or at least neutral opinion of the product). The same concept can be applied to people. When we meet someone (that we don't feel negatively about) repeatedly, we feel more and more familiarity and warmth. Studies have shown that we don't even need to have spoken to each other in order for a seed of fondness and appreciation to start growing – it's enough that we've seen each other from a distance. Hence, we can instinctively start to like people that we encounter often, who live near us, hang out in the same areas, shop in the same grocery store, or go to the same gym.

Once we have established a first connection, it is by spending more time together that we begin to create memories and overlapping frames of reference together. This contributes to a sense of belonging and the experience of an *us*. With time, a relationship without interaction eventually diminishes. At best, it can leave behind good memories and a warm feeling inside, but it is in the actual meeting between people that friendships can form and deepen.

Jeffrey Hall, professor of communication at the University of Kansas, conducted a study aiming to find out how long it takes to become friends. His rough estimate was that it takes about 90 hours of time spent together to go from being acquainted to becoming friends, and over 200 hours to go from being friends to becoming *close* friends. If you were to spend an average of two hours with somebody every time you got together, it would, according to Hall's estimate, take about a hundred social occasions to become close friends. Regardless of the accuracy of these calculations, time spent together is obviously not a guarantee of developing friendships (otherwise you would have become besties with all of your classmates or work colleagues).

Positivity

Needless to say, other than spending time together, the relationship is also affected by what we do during that time. The extent to which we are actually *there*, mentally present, and how we interact with each other is crucial for whether or not we choose to continue seeing each other. We want to spend more time with people who we feel comfortable with and who make us happy. If we express mutual appreciation, we also have a higher chance of becoming close, as opposed to if we take each other for granted, or if we complain and talk down to each other. In short, we prefer relationships that *give* rather than *take* energy from us.

Another aspect of this is that we start to like each other more when we share positive experiences. If you, for example, go to an amazing concert with a new acquaintance, chances are that you'll start to like each other more. Thus, our relationships can strengthen by trying new, fun activities, going on exciting excursions, or doing enjoyable things together, such as sharing a good meal.

Barbara Fredrickson (the psychology professor) zeroed in on this. Together with her colleagues, she has shown that positive feelings help us become more aware of and susceptible to our surroundings. We can more easily shift our focus from ourselves, and for example take notice of circumstances such as our friend got a new haircut or looks sad. This increases the chance of connection.

Similarity

If you take a minute to consider which people you like to spend time with, it will probably be clear that you are drawn to those who are 'like-minded' – people with whom you share lifestyle, interests and values. The experience of being on the same wavelength is central to friendship. We want to feel understood, and that is facilitated by similar thought patterns and having a similar perception of the world.

If you meet someone at a social event who is thirty years older or younger than you and has for you a completely incomprehensible political view, and the only thing you seem to have in common is randomly being seated next to each other, it can be hard to see how the two of you could become friends. Now imagine that, at that same event, you instead start talking to someone around your age, with the same values and frames of reference. You are drawn to the same types of people, do similar things in your free time, and your everyday lives seem to consist of the same ingredients. Besides it being easier for the two of you to understand each other, you are probably more willing to have further shared experiences. It's as if you have a head start on friendship in an emotional as well as practical way.

However, people with different views of the world, different hobbies and abilities than us, can expand our lives and sometimes even compensate for our own shortcomings. Spending time with someone who is different from yourself can open up to new ways of being and thinking. You can learn new things and experience new aspects of yourself that you may not even have known that you possessed. Although it is less common for people who seemingly don't have much in common to become close friends, there are several instances which prove it is possible. How do they do it? Perhaps the important question isn't whether or not we *are* alike, but whether or not we are able to *find* similarities and common ground – even when there initially don't appear to be any.

Reciprocity

Feelings of justice are deeply rooted in people. Those of us who have grown up with siblings know this, after countless dinners when the most important thing wasn't the taste of the dessert, but whether we got as much of it as the rest of the pack. It's easy to be generous towards friends who are generous back. However, if someone who you know is financially well-off insists on splitting the restaurant bill down to the last penny, you will probably be less inclined to pay for the next round of beers. In general, we extend our hand to the same extent that we perceive others to extend theirs. This principle, that there is balance between giving and taking in long-term friendships, is often referred to as the 'reciprocity norm'.

What needs to be balanced is what we consider to be valuable. The 'currency' can vary and be anything from material gifts to favours to emotional support. One kind of gift can be reciprocated with another. Emotional support can be reciprocated by helping someone move. The important thing is that both parties find the exchange to be fairly balanced over time. If the balance starts to fail, it usually leads to one of two situations – either the person less invested in nurturing the relationship starts to get their act together, or the other person who has invested a lot eventually tires and decreases their commitment.

Consequently, friendships rarely remain asymmetric for very long. This was also an interesting finding in Oswald's study about long-term friendship: regardless of how close the friends were (best friends, close friends or just acquaintances) they matched each other in the number of behaviours that promote friendship. Both parties reported equal levels of effort and contribution from themself and their friend.

However, it can be foolish to have an exaggerated focus on this give-and-take balance. An economic viewpoint where we make a mental note of every service and reciprocal service is hardly beneficial to the friendship. In psychological studies where the participants were told to think in such transactional terms, the researchers found that it led to more self-centred focus and less connection.

Yet another aspect of the norm of reciprocity that can be a disadvantage is that we can feel stressed when someone gives us something, whether it be material gifts, favours or compliments. It can even lead us to decline something that we actually appreciate. We may refuse a colleague's offer to pay for our lunch or apologise when a stranger waits and holds a door open for us while we're still 30 feet away. But to wholeheartedly receive can also be considered a gift to the giver, since it feels a lot better to give to someone who really appreciates it than to someone who hesitantly accepts and becomes stressed about immediately having to return the favour.

Loyalty

How does it feel when no one comes to your aid when you really need help? Or if no one has time to hang out and listen to you when you've just been dumped? We feel trust and want to spend time with friends who are there for us and show that they care. Social psychological experiments have shown that we are more inclined to like another person when we have done them a favour. Watering a friend's plants or taking care of their dog can result in you feeling a greater appreciation for that person, besides it being a way of showing that you value your relationship.

If someone breaks an agreement (without good reason), it erodes your trust and you can feel devalued and unimportant, but how we respond to 'loyalty breaches' depends on the context. If we know that someone generally has an easy-going attitude towards agreements it can be easier to overlook, compared to if that same unreliable person demands strict loyalty from others. What's important is that we feel prioritised by our friends and that we perceive that they, to the best of their ability, are willing to do us favours and sometimes make sacrifices for our sake.

How are pearls of connection created?

We have now discussed five factors that characterise 'the string' in strong friendships: *Time together, positivity, similarity, reciprocity* and *loyalty*. It can be tempting to think that we can *deepen* our relationships just by replenishing these ingredients. In many cases this is likely true. But deeper intimacy is not automatically created by spending more time together, having fun together or helping each other. If this were the case, we would all have deep relationships with, for example, our friendly colleagues, supportive parents or our friends from the football team. The factors that we have discussed thus far create good conditions for lasting friendships, but what does it take to create moments of close connection? Is there some kind of formula to forming the pearls in our string of pearls metaphor?

Generating closeness

In an attempt to understand what generates a feeling of closeness, psychology professor Arthur Aron at the Stony Brook University (USA) created a simple but powerful experiment that drew a lot of attention. Aron's hypothesis was that the degree of mutual transparency and vulnerability (for example sharing personal experiences, thoughts and feelings) is crucial to how close people perceive themselves to be. To measure the degree of closeness he developed the 'Inclusion of Other in the Self Scale'.

Circle the image that best describes your (A) relationship with person B

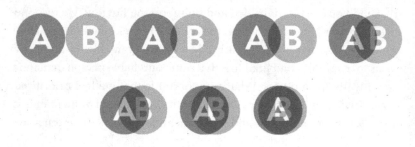

In 1997, Aron tested his hypothesis by pairing up strangers and letting them take turns to answer thirty-six questions in areas that grew increasingly personal and exposing, for example 'What would a perfect day be like for you?' and 'When was the last time you cried?' (The rest of the questions can be found in Appendix 2 at the end of the book.) The result showed that the participants who answered these questions during their 45 minutes together felt a stronger and closer bond (a greater 'overlap', measured with the scale above) compared to those who had just chatted for the same amount of time. Surprisingly, some of the participants felt as close, or closer, to their dialogue partner than to anyone else in their lives.

The spiral of openness and trust

Openness and vulnerability appear to be important ingredients in establishing closeness. However, you may not want to be completely open with just anyone. It can feel (and by all means be) much too risky to open up and expose yourself when you don't know how it will be received by the other person.

OPENNESS   **TRUST**

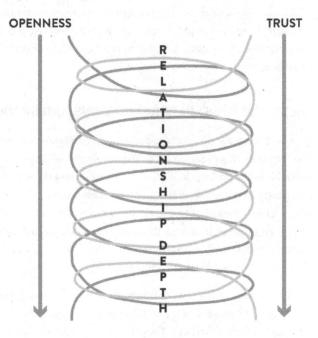

R
E
L
A
T
I
O
N
S
H
I
P

D
E
P
T
H

Anders Wendelheim, organisational consultant and doctor of psychology at Stockholm University, has illustrated this in a model that he calls the spiral of openness and trust, which we have simplified in the image above. It illustrates how openness and trust are connected and dependent on each other. Wendelheim also emphasises an important difference between the two concepts: *Openness* is something that we can voluntarily control, whereas *trust* is hard to influence directly. It is rather a consequence of someone daring to open up and having that be well received by others. The more that happens, the more trust is built.

Sometimes we get stuck. When we feel scared and insecure, we tend to be less open: 'Before I say how I feel I need to know that you're not going to judge me.' If your friend says the same, you won't get anywhere. But, if one of you is brave enough to open up a little more than the established trust at that point, it can be like putting a key into a lock. If the openness is met with understanding and warmth, it's like turning the key, and – using another metaphor – a positive, relationship-deepening spiral can be created. A relationship can move up and down the spiral over time, but once you have reached a certain depth it is usually easier to return to that level again.

OPENNESS AND TRUST IN ORGANISATIONS AND GROUPS

Openness and trust don't just characterise interpersonal closeness, but can also promote cooperation and productivity in larger groups. As mentioned in the preface, in 2015, Google published the results of an extensive study about what made some of their teams more efficient than others. Over a period of two years, they observed 180 teams. What they concluded was that it was *not* the co-workers' individual attributes and abilities that best explained which teams were successful, but rather how they conversed and treated each other within the group.

Successful teams are characterised by the members knowing that they can pose questions, ask for help, and come with suggestions without being belittled or declared stupid. They dare to voice deviating opinions, give each other feedback, and admit their mistakes, since they trust that they will be taken seriously and be treated with respect.

A-B-A – a formula for close connection

The psychology researchers Harry Reis (at the University of Rochester) and Phillip Shaver (University of California) compiled a large amount of research about relationships into a well-grounded scientific model that they call 'The Interpersonal Process Model of Intimacy'. The model, which was published in 1988, describes what happens in moments of close connection or, in other words, how a pearl is created. The model will henceforth be described with the formula 'A-B-A', as follows:

Person **A** shares something personal and shows herself vulnerable.

Person **B** answers in an understanding, accepting and kind manner.

Person **A** perceives person **B**'s answer as understanding, accepting and kind.

The more both parties mutually open up and thereafter perceive that they are met with understanding, acceptance and kindness, the closer they feel.

Two examples:

Katarina tells her two colleagues, Adam and Jennifer, that she feels comfortable with them and likes working with them. Adam and Jennifer show that they are genuinely happy to hear that and thank her for telling them. They then proceed to say that Katarina is a strong reason why they've chosen to work in this particular team. Katarina perceives that her openness is met in a kind way. It makes Katarina feel closer to Adam and Jennifer, and this increases her willingness to express similar things with them in the future.

Agnes opens up to Charlotte about having a rough time after recently being left by her partner. She doesn't feel that she wants tips or advice, but mostly just wants to talk about it. Charlotte puts aside what she is doing and faces Agnes. She shows clearly with her entire body language that she wants to listen attentively. Agnes feels that she is being taken seriously and that she can express her feelings without being interrupted. She trusts Charlotte. Charlotte cries a few tears while listening to Agnes and shows that she is touched. Agnes feels even closer to her, and feels empowered to share more difficult topics with her in the future.

We humans may be complex beings, but in some ways we are quite simple. When we notice that a certain behaviour in a given situation leads to something desirable, the probability increases that we will repeat the behaviour under similar circumstances in the future. This is a well-established psychological phenomenon, and it is referred to as the *reinforcement* of behaviour.

The A-B-A-model is, of course, a simplified reflection of reality – for example, our social interactions with friends are rarely so temporally linear, and the role distribution varies by the second. Yet simplifying what happens can make it easier to navigate the complexity. We can increase the chances of bringing about more moments of deeper connection, which in turn can be a crucial part of how the relationship continues to develop. Social interactions that are characterised by these A-B-A-interactions are beneficial to all parties. Brain imaging studies have shown that when we share something vulnerable with someone and experience the response we receive as a validating one, the brain's reward system is activated. Several studies have also shown that the occurrence of A-B-A is strongly correlated with how satisfied people are in their relationships. In other words: The more you and your friend mutually engage in this kind of give and take, the higher the chances of you liking each other and being comfortable in each other's company.

In summary

Lasting friendships are characterised by positivity, similarity, reciprocity and loyalty. They are also distinguished by spending time together. However, the depth of the connection may vary from one moment to the next. The 'pearl' moments of close connection arise when we are brave enough to be open and vulnerable and then are met in a way that we perceive as understanding, accepting and kind. When this happens, it is easier to relax, lower our guard and open up even more. The probability that we want to see each other again increases, more 'pearls' are added, and the bond of friendship grows stronger. We summarise the formula for close connection as A-B-A, and in later chapters we will zero in on the different components.

CHAPTER 3
The friendship map

Oscar rarely meets new people. At work, he meets the same colleagues every day and, unfortunately, he doesn't have a lot in common with them. He and his partner go to couples' dinners every now and then, which is usually nice, but Oscar can't deny that he feels socially starved.

During the summers of his school years, he and a few friends had a tradition of going away to a cabin together. Oscar loved how they used to hang out around the dinner table and talk for hours after each meal, but also how they could just take it easy together. He remembers how relaxed and natural it felt to just lie silently in the grass and be lazy.

Recently, when Oscar was out walking the dog, he bumped into one of his old friends, Adam, who he used to hang out with at the cabin. Both were equally surprised to see each other. They had a lot to talk about, and as it turned out, Adam had recently moved back into town after a few years of living in another city. Oscar felt exhilarated by the meeting and thought that this was a great opportunity to reconnect.

A month later, nothing had happened. Oscar thought about Adam once in a while, but doubted that it would be a good idea for him to try to reignite their friendship. Would Adam even be interested in getting together again?

Should Oscar just let go of old traditions and accept that the past is in the past, that it will never be like 'before'? Or should he send a text message to his old friend, hoping to create something new? Many of us can relate to Oscar's dilemma. When we move to a new city, begin a new, demanding job, or start a family, we can unintentionally lose touch with our friends. Several years can pass before we wake up and realise that we have long neglected something that we truly value.

This chapter contains a number of practical ideas for how you can get past common obstacles in order to gain a better social life, initiate new friendships and resume old ones. You will also be guided through a process of creating a friendship map to help you figure out what friendships you're missing or what you might want more of, and to help you take the steps towards fulfilment. Taking a moment to stop and reflect upon your social life can counteract the risk of you one day waking up to find that you haven't lived the life that you wanted.

DO YOU FEEL LONELY?

Some who make the friendship map will be reminded of all the wonderful friends who enrich their lives. Others will become painfully aware that they are lacking satisfactory relationships. If you feel very lonely and have felt that way for a long time, it can be good to know that you are not alone in feeling this way. Loneliness is a *public health issue* which means that it needs to be addressed on a societal level. However, it can certainly be important to consider what you yourself can do. For starters, it can be good to think about the reasons behind your loneliness. Have you spent your time on other matters and deprioritised friendship? Have you perhaps moved to a new city, entered a new community, become unemployed, left a relationship or lost some other important context? Do you lack the skills of connecting with others, or have you been held back by strong fears?

Most people are dependent upon feeling socially involved in order to feel well. We need some kind of context or other community – a job, a movie club, a group of people you work out with, or a family. If we are alone and only have ourselves to think about, our thoughts tend to become gloomy and we lose energy. This can sometimes throw us into a downward spiral, where we draw back and disengage instead of getting out of our own space and our own thoughts.

If you're stuck in a spiral like this, it can be hard to get out on your own. If you feel that you need more help than this book can offer, we recommend that you talk to someone. Sessions with a psychologist at your local health centre or at a private clinic can help. There are also books on how to overcome loneliness, one being *The Loneliness Cure* by Kory Floyd, PhD in Communications, which contains many helpful ideas.

Reflection exercise: The friendship map

Purpose: To get an overview of your friendship situation, how you would want it to be and which steps you can take to develop it in that direction
Time required: 15–45 minutes
Method: Writing

1. *Map out your network.*
   Get out a blank piece of paper and write down the names of your friends in a way that gives you an overview. If you want, you can include the names of acquaintances that could potentially become your friends. Use your phone or your social media accounts if you find it hard to remember those who are in your network. The map can be portrayed in several different ways, but here are a few suggestions:

   - You can write a simple list.
   - You can write your name in the middle and place your friends' names at different distances away from your own, depending on how close you feel to each person.
   - You can form groups of people in a way that feels appropriate, for example by listing new friends and acquaintances in the top left corner, old friends in the right corner, work friends in the bottom left, friends from another context in the right corner, and so on.

● You can create a friendship tree by drawing a large tree with roots and branches. Place your closest and oldest friend(s) at the roots. At the top, in the branches, you place acquaintances or new friends with whom you are not very close. At the tree trunk you place friends and acquaintances that are somewhere in between.

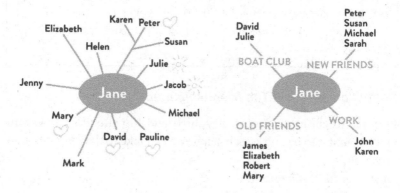

1. Write down your thoughts.

a) Take a moment to think about what the friendship map shows.

- Does this give you any new insights about your network?
- Can you see if you have mostly old friends or new friends?
- Do you have friends from one context or from several?

b) Do you see anything that you would like to change?
The following questions may help:

- How satisfied are you with how many friends you have?
- How satisfied are you with how many close and superficial friendships you have?
- Is there any kind of friendship that you are lacking?
- Is there some characteristic or value in your friendships that you would like to have more of?
- Is there anyone or several people that you would like to be closer to?

2. Map out your friendship habits.

Try to get an overview of your friendship habits by writing down how, and with whom, you have spent *the last few months*. Contemplate this on your own or use the questions below and take notes. If it's hard to remember what you have been doing, maybe your calendar can help.

- *How often* have you spent time with or been in contact with friends?
- *Which* friends have you spent time with or been in contact with?
- When you have spent time with friends, *what have you done together*?

3. Write down your thoughts.

Now take a few minutes to think about the habits you have clarified. How satisfied are you with them? Is there anything you'd like to change? The following questions can help you clarify what you like, and become aware of what you may want to have more (or less) of:

- With which friends or under what circumstances are you the most content and comfortable?
- With which friends or under what circumstances are you less content and comfortable?
- What contributes to you finding social interactions meaningful?

● If you haven't spent time with friends in a long time – what used to contribute to meaningful social interactions for you?

4. *Write down which changes you would like to make and which steps you can take.*

From that answer, write down what (if anything) you would like to change or develop. Then, try to think of and write down *actual steps* that you can take to get closer to your goal. What can you *do* to nurture or develop your friendships? If you find it hard to think of anything, you can follow the instructions in the box on the next page. You can also keep reading the ideas and advice that follow in the rest of the chapter, before perhaps coming back to your friendship map to make your steps even more concrete.

PROBLEM-SOLVING – TAKE A STEP IN THE RIGHT DIRECTION

If you find it difficult to know how to obtain the friendships you desire, this problem-solving method may help.

1. *Choose an area in which you want to progress.*

Start off by choosing an area in which you want to progress. From there, we suggest that you formulate your desire in 'I would like to' terms, for example:

'I would like to have more friends.'

'I would like to spend more, casual time with X.'

'I would like to do new things with my friends.'

2. *Brainstorm on which steps you could take.*

Write down all the things you could do (or refrain from doing) to move in your desired direction. Try not to judge your ideas – judgements obstruct your creativity. Instead, let all kinds of ideas come out, even those that you may not believe in or that you consider to be ridiculous or weird – it will help your imagination.

3. *Pick one or two steps.*

When you have thought of a number of conceivable steps you can start to assess them: Which ones do you find the most promising?

Circle the ideas that you like, or write a plus or a minus next to each one.

4. *Create an action plan.*

Perhaps you can already, after just a few minutes, take one of the steps (or several) that you have chosen, for example 'Send a text message.' If that's the case, go for it! Maybe it's harder than that to get what you want. In that case, we suggest that you do the following in order to lower the threshold for action:

A. Express yourself as *clearly* as possible, so that you know exactly what it actually entails to take the step or steps that you want to take. For example, it's more concrete to write 'Text Lisa and suggest a lunch date' than 'Contact Lisa.'

B. If needed, *break down* the step into smaller portions. For example, 'Book a cabin in the countryside' can be broken down into 1) Ask X what area they rented a cabin in last year. 2) Look for cabins in that area. 3) Check available dates. And so on.

C. Schedule *when* you are going to take the step (or steps) by, for example, writing it in your calendar.

5. *Foresee possible obstacles.*

Ask yourself if there is anything that could prevent you from doing as you have planned. If so, specify the obstacle and think about what you could do to get around it.

6. *Execute your action plan!*

7. *Repeat the procedure.*

If this was helpful, and you think you could benefit from working on more areas, repeat the procedure starting from step 1.

Change isn't always comfortable

We often do things (or refrain from doing things) to avoid something difficult, uncomfortable or painful. Oscar, whom we introduced in the beginning of this chapter, is reluctant to contact Adam, even though he knows it could boost his wellbeing. In the moment, it's more comfortable for him to scroll through the news feed on his phone than to formulate a text message – he avoids difficult thoughts such as 'He may not even answer.'

Similarly, we can guess that Oscar would probably feel a slight resistance towards doing the friendship map exercise. The easiest thing he can do is to just get on with his life without taking any risks. However, he would miss the opportunity of getting a better overview of his friendships and what he can do to improve them.

In this chapter, perhaps you will realise that there is a *gap* between your desired and your actual situation. This realisation can hurt. If so, can you see the pain as a signal that it's time to do something about it? Maybe it can motivate you to try to make decisions that are more in line with your desire for change.

We call the continuum line below the *Value Line*. It illustrates how we can choose to move in one of two directions. When we move forward, towards what we value and want more of, it's common to initially experience some degree of doubt, discomfort or concern. If we move backwards, we can avoid those thoughts and feelings short term, but after a while we realise that we're not living our lives as we want. We're still longing to move forward, but are stuck in short-term strategies to avoid discomfort.

Avoiding discomfort
For example:
Watching a funny clip on your phone instead of contacting a friend.

Following your longing
For example:
Having the courage to face what's difficult and continuing to take steps towards what's valuable.

Keeping busy to avoid feeling discomfort. Brooding about whether or not someone likes you instead of reaching out and making contact.

Moving towards what you want even if it feels scary.

Reaching out to someone even though it makes you feel vulnerable.

IF YOU ARE REJECTED

We can never control how others are going to react. Maybe you will get a no when you reach out to make contact according to your friendship map. You may be disappointed. It can be wise to prepare coping strategies if the risk feels high.

In the worst-case scenario (when moving in the direction of your desires), how do you think you would instinctively react? Would it be to withdraw, start accusing, break contact, say something mean or something else?

In the best of all worlds, how would you act in the worst-case scenario? Would you be understanding and not attack the person who rejected you? Would you tell yourself that it's OK, or remind yourself of someone who likes you and sees your good qualities?

What else could help you if the worst came to the worst? Do you have any advice for yourself? Would it, for example, be helpful to talk to a friend, meet up with some people that can support you, do something that lifts you up and strengthens you?

How to strengthen *existing* bonds

You will now receive a smorgasbord of ideas, inspiration and practical tips that can help you strengthen your existing friendships. How can you, for example, see each other more frequently? How can you enrich time spent together?

Make new plans right away

When you and an old friend are saying goodbye after a fun evening in each other's company, you both agree that you want to get together again and say: 'We have to do this again – soon!' Of course, we can sometimes say things like that just to be polite, but other times we really mean it. Yet, it often takes too long before we get around to actually doing it. Something as simple as making preliminary plans about a time and maybe even a place for your next get-together can be the detail that ensures that years won't pass before you see each other again.

Set up recurring get-togethers

Aside from recurring get-togethers actually increasing the chances of seeing friends more frequently, the knowledge that we will get together again constitutes a secure foundation for the friendship. The relationship develops a 'built-in' continuation. In order to obtain this you can, for example, start a book, movie or game club, take up a new sport with a friend (for example playing badminton every or every other week), or put together a soccer team with friends. Perhaps you and a friend can share a subscription or a season pass – or just decide to always go to certain games or shows together.

Set aside time for socialising with friends

If you don't have a specific person or activity in mind, but still want to create more space for socialising, one suggestion is to set aside time in your calendar, just as you do for other activities that you want to prioritise (like exercising or studying). For example, you can make Tuesday evenings (or, if you have a full schedule, the first Tuesday of every month) 'friend evenings', that you keep free from other activities and instead reserve to spend time with friends.

Break habitual patterns

If you feel like you're stuck in a rut with a friend, it can be due to spending too much time in the same place or usually doing the same things. Changing your environment and activity can inspire unexpected qualities – just think about how differently you act at work compared to at home, or in your childhood home compared to at a dance class. Maybe next time, you and your friend can get together at a spa? If you're used to getting together at a cafe or restaurant maybe do some arts and crafts or cook together at home instead?

Start projects together

One way of having recurring get-togethers and at the same time breaking habitual patterns, is to create some kind of project together. Here are some ideas:

- Take on a mission (like having a picnic in every park of the city, reading every book by a certain author, or seeing every movie by a certain director).
- Learn something new together (for example a language or a musical instrument).
- Take a class together (dance, gardening, art or photography).
- Start a band.
- Join a club together.

Lower the bar

It can be rewarding to do new things with each other, but spending meaningful time together doesn't always have to be so exotic or grand. It's easy to underestimate how much there is to gain from *briefer* moments of connection. You can, for example, take a 15-minute walk or just give a friend a call to say 'Hi, I only have five minutes, but I was thinking of you and wanted to say hello and see how you're doing!' Both in the moment and in the long run, a short moment of connection is better than no connection.

Other than lowering the bar of ambition for *how long* we get together, we also ought to lower the bar of *what we do*. For instance – is it completely necessary to cook a fancy meal every time you invite your friend over? Even though you may enjoy cooking delicious food, it's probably less fun if the task of creating a three-course meal stands between you and the get-together with your dearly missed friend. If the purpose is to take part in each other's lives, that can just as easily be done over a bowl of cereal and has the advantage of being more likely to actually happen. Don't let perfection stand in your way – instead, take advantage of the opportunities of simple meetings.

Do things you already do – together!
Perhaps you and your friend can start exercising together, or go grocery shopping together if you live near one another? If you both work from home, maybe you can sit and work together? Or why not spend time together when one of you has laundry day or is cleaning out their closet?

A more common tip is to set breakfast or lunch dates with old friends and potential new friends who live or work nearby. This can be a nice way to spend time together, seeing as most of us always eat breakfast and lunch anyway. It doesn't involve any advance planning and we don't need to deprioritise other activities. Suggesting brief and unpretentious get-togethers can be easier than, for example, asking a busy friend to set aside an entire Friday evening.

Low energy doesn't have to be a drawback
'Sorry, I'm feeling a little tired. Do you think we can get together next week instead?' Even if it's natural to withdraw when you're feeling tired or low, it can also be freeing to let go of the notion that you have to be or feel a certain way. If you only socialise with others when you're at your best and have a high energy level, you can fall into the trap of thinking that others only want to see those sides of you – and that they wouldn't accept you when you're feeling low. However, if you can let others in, regardless of whether you're feeling sad, relaxed, anxious, tired, wired up, grumpy, goofy or hungover, you open up to more opportunities for connection. It also paves the way for a relationship which includes more sides of yourself. Another aspect is that our

mood often changes when we connect. Maybe you can relate to feeling down but, when deciding to get together with a trusted friend anyway, noticing your mood improves with the visit.

Spend longer periods of time together

As we mentioned earlier, brief get-togethers are better than no get-togethers. However, when we get an opportunity to spend longer periods of time together, we can strengthen our bonds in additional ways. Imagine the difference between meeting a friend for a cup of coffee compared to going away for a weekend together. More time together usually leads to seeing more sides of each other, and allows us to engage in more profound and intimate conversations. If we see each other when we're free and maybe in a 'vacation mood', chances are that we'll be more present and allow ourselves to be more spontaneous and exploratory than when we get together during a weekday and have to keep track of time.

Offer your help

Just as it can be strengthening for a relationship to *ask* for help, it can also be nourishing to *offer* help to others. Perhaps there's something that you're good at that you could help your friend with? Maybe you're great with computers and your friend has some trouble with his or hers? Maybe you could help your friend to build a new bookshelf or lay a new floor? Refurbish a chair or proofread an essay? Maybe you have something to lend – for example your car, or why not that book they want to read?

How to find new friends

The world is full of interesting people. If you want to make new acquaintances and friends, the following tips may be helpful.

Talk to strangers

Imagine the following scenario: Two strangers approach you on the train platform one morning. They are researchers and wonder if you would like to participate in a study of how people are impacted by social contact. All you have to do is answer this question:

> *How do you think you would feel if, during your train ride, you were to chat with a fellow passenger of your choice, compared to if you were to do just as you usually do?*

Nicholas Epley, professor of behavioural science at the University of Chicago, asked people to answer this and other similar questions in several different studies. Many people replied that they would feel awkward and that the person they talked to would feel even more uncomfortable. In other words, they considered contact with strangers to be a lose-lose situation.

But what *actually* happened when people did this? In repeated experiments, Nicholas Epley and his team of researchers asked randomly selected people to make contact with unknown passengers. About 40 per cent of the participants initially guessed that they wouldn't even be able to strike up a conversation. However, 100 per cent of all attempts succeeded. Furthermore, time and time again, the result was that the people doing this felt significantly happier afterwards than those who were asked to keep to themselves and act as usual.

In other experiments, the same team of researchers found that it wasn't just the people initiating the contact that became happier, but also those who were being contacted. Other researchers found that extraverts and introverts were equally positively affected by talking to new people. However, those who were introverts were more likely to *guess* that they would feel uncomfortable.

Probably better liked than you think

Psychologist Erica Boothby and her colleagues at Cornell University have found that people systematically underestimate how much other people like them. In an experiment where the researchers let strangers chat briefly, the participants afterwards guessed that the other person liked them less than they actually did. This phenomenon is called *the liking gap*. Unfortunately, this illusion appears to be persistent – we continue to believe that our acquaintances like us less than they actually do, even after having seen each other several times. In a similar way, we underestimate how happy we make others by showing our appreciation or giving them compliments.

Just saying hello or making small talk with a stranger seems to have a greater impact than many of us believe. These kinds of brief encounters may not change our lives, but they can make our everyday life more pleasant by turning dull or lonely moments into more rewarding ones. Chances are high that it will be a win-win situation, and if we're lucky, it can be the beginning of a new friendship.

Fish in the right pond

By spending time in contexts that are dear to your heart you will most likely find intriguing people who share your interests and values. You can also increase your chances of finding new friends by spending more time with people you already know and like, since they, in turn, will most likely have friends that you may 'click' with. For similar reasons, there are advantages in spending time in contexts that are geographically close to you. To increase the chances of finding new contacts, you can, for example, during your vacation choose to take an interesting class in your area as opposed to travelling to a remote city. Below are a few examples of 'fishing ponds' where you can hopefully get a good catch:

- Join a non-profit organisation where you can volunteer.
- Find and sign up for a class, for example in a study group or at a community college.
- Search for the words 'friendship dating' online and you'll find several apps and websites that may be of interest. For example, there's Meetup, which has different groups arranged by interests and city. There are, of course, also other digital meeting forums for finding new friends.
- If you have colleagues that you find interesting, you can suggest doing some kind of activity together, like having lunch at a restaurant or meeting up for an after-work drink.

- Go friendship-fishing online. For instance, you can post an open question on social media asking if someone wants to get together. Try to be concrete. For example, you can write: 'I'm having lunch at Restaurant X tomorrow at noon, does anyone want to join me?'
- If you see that an acquaintance has shown an interest in the same event as you (for example on social media), you can contact them and ask if they want to get together for the event.
- Become acquainted with neighbours or people whose paths often cross yours. It could be parents at your child's day-care centre, or an acquaintance that you often pass on your way to work.
- Ask your family and friends to help you by suggesting people that they think you would like. Maybe you can even ask them to arrange an occasion when you can meet?

Do your thing and attract others

Preschool teachers often encourage lonely children to ask other kids if they can join in their game. Another strategy is to encourage them to simply start doing what they think is fun on their own. When a child has gotten out his favourite building blocks and built an amazing fairy-tale scene, the probability is high that other kids will become interested and want to join. In a similar way, you increase your chances of attracting others by doing activities that give you joy and energy. Maybe someone will be inspired and want to join your projects, whether it be tending to the garden of your apartment building, having a barbecue in the courtyard, or taking walks on your lunch breaks.

Seize opportunities

If you meet someone that you find interesting and that you'd like to get to know better, be proactive. Don't settle for 'I hope we see each other again some time.' Instead, at least ask for some kind of contact information. A simple thing like that can be crucial. It can also be helpful to suggest a time for your next get-together as early as possible. Instead of just letting your aspiration linger in the air, make a habit of establishing it in a distinct suggestion, such as: 'How about having lunch together again next Wednesday?'

Update your friendship map

Another suggestion is to set aside five minutes every now and then to add new names to your friendship map. It can be people you've encountered in your everyday life and that you want to get to know better – perhaps a neighbour that you've just said hi to, or a colleague that you spontaneously started talking to during a coffee break. It can be people you've never spoken to, but that you've noticed on social media – someone who writes interesting posts or that you know hangs out in your area. Circle two to five names (the ones that you feel the most drawn to) and think about a few things you could do to arrange an opportunity to meet them. Be as distinct as you can when making your plans. For example, 'Call Sarah and ask if she wants to go see a movie' is more distinct than 'Contact Sarah', and usually increases the odds of actually doing it.

Listen to your heart instead of 'shoulds' and 'musts'

Perhaps you've realised there are people you see regularly that you, quite frankly, don't get anything out of – maybe you have grown apart or you've never actually had much in common. Maybe the relationship is lacking in reciprocity. If you haven't really valued the friendship, you probably haven't felt motivated to try to remedy the shortcomings.

Sometimes, we can do both ourselves and others a favour by being more sincere about which relationships we want to invest our time in. Think about if you have any relationships which drain your energy but which you feel obligated to maintain. What could you do to be more true to yourself? Could you make an effort to become closer to that person, or maybe raise an issue you've been avoiding? Or is the relationship ultimately not good for you? Many of us have a hard time saying no to others, which can explain why we continue to spend time with people even though we don't get much out of the relationship. To go back to the Value Line mentioned earlier, it's often easier to avoid the discomfort. However, saying 'no' to someone almost always means that we're saying 'yes' to something else, and could be making space for more rewarding relationships.

Our first piece of advice is to reflect on which people you feel like spending time with. If you only have one evening per week to socialise, think twice before you accept an invitation to a meagre after-work event with distant colleagues. Instead, invite the new, exciting neighbour to join you for a walk. You can also be a little more systematic. As we mentioned in the section above, you can use your friendship map as a starting point. Identify which people you would like to get together with more often, and then think about specific things that you can do to get closer to them. By personally taking the initiative to socialise with those you really want to spend time with, you reduce the risk of getting stuck in the habit of saying yes to people who really want to see you, but who you yourself feel less eager to meet.

In summary

The world is full of people who could potentially become a future friend. The next person you meet at a party may inspire you to adopt a completely new career. Someone you come across in a class may be your anchor in a future life crisis. If we give people the time and create the environment to become closer, an acquaintance could become a friend and a friend could become a best friend.

The exercises in this chapter have given you the opportunity to clarify the difference between your reality and what friendships you're craving. Hopefully, you've also gotten some ideas about things you can do, big or small, to minimise the potential gap. If you are ready to take a step or two forward on your Value Line, initially it may feel a bit uncomfortable. Yet, when we take small steps outside of our comfort zone, our tolerance tends to grow. You can of course put the whole thing off. You can wait for a better occasion, or for change to come to you. Or you could skip the wait. You can take a small step forward anytime and see what happens.

CHAPTER 4
The interpersonal skills you have acquired

As a child, Karen could rarely trust her parents – they made promises but, when push came to shove, they forgot their promises, letting other things get in the way. Now, as an adult, it can be difficult for Karen when she makes plans with friends. She needs to know that they will do as they've promised, and it's important to her that others show up on time. Since Karen began to see the connection between her previous experiences and her reaction patterns, she has relaxed judgement of herself and her friends. Now she understands her compulsion to double or triple check meeting times, and when someone is late she has learned that they are not completely unreliable. Since Karen has shared this with her closest friends, it has become easier for them to be patient with her when she falls back into the old habits she's trying to break.

How have you become who you are today? How is your *now* marked by your *then*? Everything we think, feel and do is shaped by our experiences earlier in life, in combination with our unique set of genes. We are born into this world under different conditions and, with our genetic backpack in tow, we go through life to form relationships, which in turn shape us. When we are aware of our *strengths* we can use them more actively and, by being aware of our *weaknesses*, we can become more humble and open to learning. In this chapter we will explore what you have learned about relationships through your past, and what skills you have (or lack) today.

We do as we have learned

When we become close to other people, with or without romantic intentions, we think and act based on what we believe to be true about relationships. Some of us experienced as children that we *can* trust those who are close to us – that they are there for us, both physically and emotionally. This experience gives a basic sense of security, so that later in life we can build solid relationships rather easily. We are neither afraid of intimacy, nor are we afraid of conflicts or of being alone (in developmental psychology, this is referred to as a *secure attachment style*). Some of us, however, have learned that we *cannot* trust those who are close to us. Perhaps our parents struggled with mental health issues, emotional problems, were distant, inconsistent or manipulative. Later in life, in our adult relationships, fears can be triggered through an unconscious expectation that we will be treated as we were during childhood (this is called *insecure attachment style*). Regardless of how we started our lives, the good news is we can change our patterns and relearn how to have secure attachments.

By becoming more aware of how we are wired, and how our past affects our present, we can take greater accountability for, and be more understanding of, ourselves. In turn, we increase our possibility of learning from our mistakes and becoming better at managing our relationships. Recognition of how we are affected by our experiences can also make us more understanding towards others, who are equally shaped by their past, which differs from our own. So, when a friend breaks up with one partner after another over the slightest issue in the relationship, we can suspect that there are underlying reasons other than them being immature.

Perhaps you are one of many who has fewer or more superficial friendships than you would have liked. Perhaps you, like millions of others, carry memories of loss, betrayal and destructive relationships. Even if you feel resistance towards exposing and remembering these issues, we advise you to complete the following exercise and to try to be as honest with yourself as possible.

Reflection exercise: Your relationship history[2]

Purpose: To increase your awareness of how your relationship patterns are shaped by your past
Time required: 20–60 minutes
Method: Writing, alone or with a friend

Take a closer look at your own past to increase your understanding of what in your past contributes to your current relationships. If possible, and if it feels right for you, we recommend that you do this exercise with a friend, and that you share your insights with each other.

---

2 A revised version of the exercise 'Life History', from the book *Functional Analytic Psychotherapy Made Simple*, by Gareth Holman et al. 2017.

1. *Get an overview*
a) *Draw your lifeline.*
   Start by drawing a vertical line on a blank piece of paper. At the top, there's you now, today, and at the bottom is when you were born. Mark your age in decades as in the illustration.

b) *Write down important events and circumstances.*
   The next step is to notice important events and circumstances in your social life. You don't have to write long explanations; brief key-words are enough. On the right side of the line, write things that have been mostly positive for you and, on the left side, things that have been more negative. The focus should be on relationships but, to jog your memory and to get a better overview, you can also mark other milestones (for example if you've moved, started at a new school, changed jobs, etc.). Write these things along the centre line.

2. *What do you see?*
   Now it's time to pause and reflect on what you see. The questions below can either be answered one at a time, or serve as more of an inspiration for your own exploration. If you're doing this exercise with a friend, the two of you can discuss the questions that you find the most interesting.

Reflect on your lifeline.
   a) Which of the past events and circumstances, positive or negative, have had the biggest impact on your life?
   b) In which social contexts have you felt the most secure and insecure, and what significant impact do you think those experiences have had on you?
   c) When looking back, can you see what has been easier or more difficult for you, socially? For instance, it could be building new relationships, maintaining relationships, taking up space, asking for or accepting help and support, giving or receiving criticism, etc.
   d) Can you see what has contributed to your strengths in relationships today? Can you see what has contributed to your challenges?

e) Do you have preconceived notions about others that you think can be traced back to your past? For example, it could be a belief that others mean what they say or that they are generally unreliable.

f) If you were to see your relationship history as a movie in which you played the lead role – during which episodes would you feel the most compassion for yourself?

g) Are there parts of your relationship history that you'd rather not pause and reflect on? If you were to do it anyway, how do you think it would feel?

h) Do you carry fears that can be traced back to your past? Have you, for instance, been betrayed, let down, criticised or punished in a way that you think still affects you?

i) If you could delete one event from your past that has something to do with a relationship – which would it be and why?

j) If you had the opportunity to go back in time and meet yourself during a period when you were going through a rough patch socially – what would you want to do for your former self?

We can't change our past, but we can change how we relate to it. What happens if we exchange self-criticism with nurturing understanding and compassion? The past will always be the same, but the burden we carry can be eased. Using the lifeline and the reflection exercises thus far, maybe you have found a specific theme that you would like to continue working on when it comes to friendship. Write it down and keep it in mind as you continue reading.

Become aware of your strengths and weaknesses

Throughout your life you have accumulated experiences and a variety of social skills. Some of them you may use frequently, while others are tucked away, waiting to be brought out when needed. Some social skills may need some work, while others need to be used more, simply in order to improve your relationships. Perhaps you sometimes get annoyed with people for not having adequate tools to manage their relationship with you and others.

A commonly used allegation is that 'if you're annoyed with X it's actually because you're annoyed with the same issue or quality in yourself'. Could there be some truth to this? We aren't aware of any research that confirms this statement, but a model we find useful for understanding ourselves and our triggers better is presented by the organisation Gro. The model (based on Daniel Ofman's work and here adapted further) outlines how things that annoy us and we are sensitive towards can be traced back to things we ourselves aren't very good at. Understanding this connection can help us to become less critical and more tolerant or forgiving towards others. The model also helps us to become aware of our core qualities, such as things that we're extra good at and distinguish us from others. However, too much of our core qualities could (depending on our environment and how we use them) backlash and become weaknesses.

The following two exercises aim to increase your awareness of your strengths and weaknesses, your skills and your limitations. They are not scientific tests, nor do they say anything about how you are in comparison to others. Consider them tools to obtain improved self-awareness.

Reflection exercise: Your core qualities and your hypersensitivity in relation to others

Purpose: To become aware of your strengths, weaknesses and areas for improvement
Time required: 5–20 minutes
Method: Writing

1. *Write down your core qualities.*

   Your core qualities are the characteristics that others immediately associate with you – your strengths. For example: *Creative, good listener, generous.* They come naturally to you and you may not even be aware of them, but others see them clearly. Your core qualities can be attributes that you more or less expect others to have, but often think that they lack or have too little of. The following questions can help you figure them out: What do others see and appreciate in you? What do you take for granted in yourself? What do you expect from others? You're not meant to account for all of your traits, just identify one to four qualities which immediately come to mind when reading the questions above. Write them down in the square 'core quality' below.

2. *Write down your difficulties and pitfalls.*

   When we get too much of the good (that is to say, too much of someone's core quality) in a certain context, it can clash with the needs of others. A creative person can become chaotic. A generous person can become invasive and self-effacing. Try to identify your pitfalls by answering the question: What about me (if anything) usually annoys others? Write it down in the square 'pitfalls'.

3. *Write down your challenges.*

   Your challenges are the positive opposites of your pitfalls – things you ought to be doing more of. For example, a self-sacrificing person may need to practise standing up for themselves and listening to their own needs. Someone who is used to taking up a lot of space could benefit from practising active listening and being more open to the ideas of others. The following questions can help you identify your challenges: What do you wish you had more of? What would others say that you could be better at? What do you admire in others? Write it down in the square 'challenges'.

4. *Write down what you're overly sensitive to.*

   According to this theory, we tend to be irritated with others when they do too much of what we ourselves ought to be doing more of (our challenges). For instance, a very generous person can become angry when someone else stands up for themselves and takes up space. The following questions can help you become aware of what you're overly sensitive to: What traits do you tend to dislike in others? How would you least of all want to act or be? Write it down in the square 'allergy'.

Take a look at the illustration on the next page and think about whether your hypersensitivity is somehow connected to something that you could work to improve. Maybe you can learn something from the person you're annoyed with.

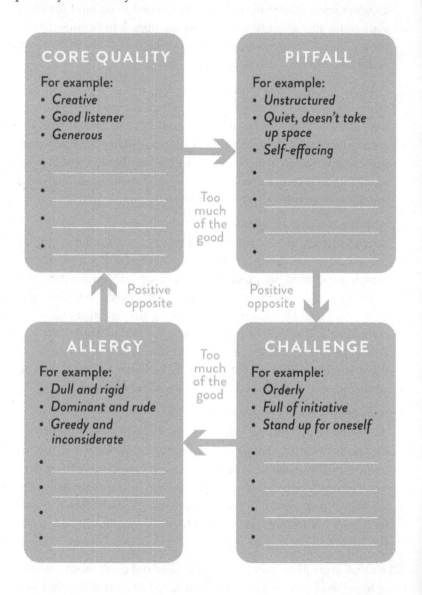

Reflection exercise: Map out your skills in promoting connection

Purpose: To get an overview of your strengths and weaknesses that are key to forming close connections with others
Time required: 10–20 minutes
Method: Writing, preferably in three different colours, alone or with a friend

In this exercise we will take a closer look at specific skills which are key to establishing connections. You will go deeper into these areas further on in the book. This inventory is the start of what can become extra helpful for you to focus on as you continue reading.

The exercise consists of fifteen claims that all describe different skills in promoting connection. The claims can – but don't need to – be assessed in three rounds, where you preferably use a different coloured pen each time.

1. Assess the claims.

First round
Answer the questions based on your own perception of your skills. When you read a claim, trust your gut feeling and assess how well it applies to you.

Second round
You grade the claims based on how you *think* a friend, or those closest to you, would assess your skills. Preferably use another colour.

Third round
Lastly, we recommend that you let a friend assess you, based on how they (honestly) perceive your skills. Preferably use a third colour.

Here is the scale:

1	2	3	4	5
Completely disagree	Mostly disagree	Partially agree	Mostly agree	Completely agree

Self-awareness (Chapter 5, Without your presence, no connection)	
I am aware of, and can identify, my feelings as they emerge in the moment.	⟷
I am aware of, and can meet, my needs as they emerge in social situations.	⟷
I can avoid automatically acting on impulses that are not beneficial to connection with others.	⟷
Awareness of others (Chapter 6, Entering your friend's world)	
I am aware of my thoughts and perception of others and can see that they are merely interpretations (and not necessarily true).	⟷
I am open and responsive to others' needs and feelings as they emerge in the moment.	⟷
Candidness and vulnerability (Chapter 7, Vulnerable and reachable)	
I can be open and allow my feelings to naturally shine through to be seen by others.	⟷

I can express what I feel, need, and want from others.	◄——————————————►
I can admit when I have made a mistake and take responsibility for it.	◄——————————————►
I can take in appreciation and kindness from others and accept their help.	◄——————————————►
Kindness and good intentions (Chapter 8, Responsiveness is key)	
I can be present with others when they experience difficult emotions.	◄——————————————►
I can show understanding and empathy for others.	◄——————————————►
I can meet the needs of others without neglecting my own.	◄——————————————►
Conflict skills (Chapter 9, Transforming conflicts)	
I can *receive* negative feedback without immediately getting defensive or putting myself down.	◄——————————————►
I can *give* negative feedback without putting others down.	◄——————————————►
I can establish boundaries and say no in a constructive way.	◄——————————————►

2. *Identify where the answers from the three rounds differ the most.*
   Now reflect on what you see. If the claims have been assessed in three rounds – are the assessments different? For which claims do the assessments differ the most? Can you think of any conceivable reasons for the disparities?

3. *Circle your main growth areas.*

   Lastly, circle three to five claims (skills) that you would like to focus on a little extra as you continue reading.

In summary

No one has walked the exact same path as you, and no one sees the world in the exact same way that you do. Your unique learning history is, for better or worse, the baggage you carry with you. The path to a desired change or development starts with awareness – becoming aware of who you are, what you carry with you, and where you want to go. We hope that the exercises in this chapter have given you a greater insight in this. Hopefully, you have also obtained an overview of the skills you may want to develop with the help of this book.

CHAPTER 5
Without your presence, no connection

Lisa and Paul, who have been close friends since high school, get together for a beer. Paul just got fired from his job and is upset. He goes on a rant and doesn't ask Lisa a single question about how she's doing. Lisa, who just came from a good workout session, is feeling great. She listens intently and relates to Paul's frustration. For a moment, she wants to interrupt and offer him a piece of advice, but she realises that's not what Paul needs right now, so she chooses to just keep listening. Her phone rings, but she ignores it. She thinks about how much she appreciates Paul and wants to support him, but his ranting goes on and on. Lisa's stomach begins to growl from hunger, and she starts feeling a little restless. She mentions that she's hungry, but Paul barely registers. Lisa gets more and more distracted by the growling in her belly and starts feeling frustrated that she's not getting any space in the conversation. Eventually, she cuts in and says: 'Paul, I do want to hear about this, but I really need to eat something soon if I'm going to have any energy to listen.' Paul feels bad: 'Oh crap, I'm sorry! I was completely in my own world. Of course, let's get something to eat. Where do you want to go?'

In Chapter 2, *A formula for friendship*, we introduced the A-B-A formula that describes what happens between two people during moments of close connection. The first step, opening up, requires being aware of what you feel, need and want in that moment. If *you* aren't in touch with yourself, it will be harder for *others* to be, and that reduces the chance of you being seen and met in a sincere way. In this chapter, we will explore how we can build a foundation for close meetings through being in touch with what we will call our *core*.

Connect with your core

Our *core* consists of what we feel, need and want *here and now*. In the example above, Lisa is aware of her bodily signals. She can interpret the situation and resists her impulses to interrupt, since she also wants to support her friend. But after a while, she gets tired of disregarding her own needs. She needs food and she also wants to feel seen by Paul. By recognising this, and also expressing what she needs and wants, she helps Paul gain insight into her experience. This opens up the way for a deeper connection between them.

Being connected to our core doesn't require a ten-day mindfulness retreat. Nor do we need to develop any esoteric skills. In fact, our core is something we all experience. The challenge is rather to repeatedly reconnect with our core. So what can help us achieve that?

Slow down

Something that generally helps our self-awareness is to *slow down*. If you fast-forward a movie clip, it's hard to notice all the details. If instead you watch it in slow motion, you will see details you won't notice at normal speed. It becomes easier to register what you feel and need when you, for instance, slow down the speed of your speech and make room for more pauses. Try playing around with this. Allow for more spaces and pauses to give yourself time to feel your core.

Allow yourself to feel, even discomfort

Social interaction doesn't just stir up positive emotions. Many of our most intense negative emotions are triggered in social contexts. For instance, without other people, we wouldn't be afraid of being rejected or excluded, and we wouldn't feel any shame. We learn from an early age to try to avoid such negative emotions. When we feel nervous, sad or irritated, we often try to distance ourselves from our feelings, instead of meeting them head on. 'Suck it up', 'be positive', and 'don't get caught up' are expressions that indicate that we *shouldn't* stop and feel too much. Instead, we smile and say that everything's great when someone asks us how we're doing. If there's an awkward silence, we desperately try to find something to say. If our friend tells us that he or she feels bad, we try to quickly wash over the sad feelings by suggesting solutions. That's understandable, but it may come at a cost. If we withhold important parts of our inner selves from ourselves and others, we miss out on sincere meetings and emotional intimacy.

A cure for this emotional evasion is to do the exact opposite, i.e., to instead *close in* on what feels unaccustomed, uncomfortable or frightening. We can *embrace* our experience, which means unconditionally accepting, fully feeling and *being* in our physical sensations and emotions.

Tom, a friend of the authors, has told us that he – both in his professional life and in his free time – used to get stuck in limiting roles and rarely felt that he could be himself. 'Instead of experiencing my feelings, I acted habitually on them. For example, I would keep talking to avoid awkward silences, or would be overly interested in the other person. It was difficult at first, but once I dared to lower my guard and allow all kinds of emotions, I noticed that I became much more present.'

If you can relate to Tom's narrative and want to practise facing your emotions, see the exercise 'Verbalise your feelings' in Appendix 1.

Reconnecting with yourself

It is not only uncomfortable feelings that make it difficult for us to connect with our core. Many other things can cloud our connection with ourselves and others – phones that ring, media feeds that grab our attention, and so on. Tom described how he practised reconnecting with himself: 'I started practising returning to my body and what I felt physically. It was as if my body became an anchor to the now. I still practise reconnecting with myself and noticing how I feel when meeting others – it helps.'

One direct way of connecting with your core is to every now and then take *micropauses*. Without trying to change anything, just briefly check in on your overall condition. Check in on your body (maybe 'tense breathing and a contraction in your stomach'), and on your mind (maybe 'tired and bored'). Feel if there's anything you need (maybe 'release your train of thought for a moment'). Below we describe this very simple method that you can use anytime and anywhere in your everyday life and during social interactions with others.

Portable tool: Micropausing

Purpose: Connecting with your core
Time required: 2–10 seconds
Method: Mentally

1. *Stop and let go of your thoughts for a moment.*
2. *Notice the overall feeling in your body right now.*
   How do your stomach and your chest feel? How is your breathing?
3. *Notice your emotional state. How do you feel? Restless?*
   At ease? Sad? Happy?
4. *Notice what's present in you at this very moment.*
   Is there something you want? Something you need?

Every time you check in on your inner self like this – even if it's just for a few seconds – you give yourself an opportunity to act more intentionally than if you had just continued on the same path without pausing to reflect. You begin to realise that you can make adjustments to your direction, guiding you to something more meaningful in the moment. Over time, this practice can have a great impact on the quality of your meetings and relationships.

When your cup is full, there's no space for others

Most people would probably agree that we become poor listeners when we feel stressed or unsafe, or maybe when we're simply tired or hungry. Paul, in this chapter's introductory example, had trouble thinking about anything other than losing his job, and it was also the only thing that he talked about. Lisa, on the other hand, was balanced and recharged with good energy after her workout session. Therefore, she had better conditions to take in more, and broader perspectives to see what was relevant for both herself and Paul.

Carrying around unsatisfied needs is like walking around with a pebble in your shoe. As long as the discomfort is there, it's difficult to think of anything other than the pebble. Usually, it's not until we remove it that we're able to expand our focus to take in what's going on inside of ourselves or within our surroundings. When we satisfy our needs, it's like removing the pebble from our shoe and creating mental space.

This idea is indirectly confirmed by experimental studies where the participants have been asked to report what they see in visual images such as the one below.

```
HHHHH
H
HHHHH
H
H
H
```

A person who is stressed or depressed orients towards details ('a bunch of H:s'), while a person who is happy or content tends to see the bigger picture ('an F and a bunch of H:s'). The psychology professor Barbara Fredrickson, whom we mentioned earlier, has shown that positive feelings help us open and broaden our attention, and that this helps us create and maintain contact with others. She calls it to *broaden and build*. The fact that our own mood and wellbeing not only affect ourselves, but also our opportunities of closer connection with others, is therefore yet another reason to start taking care of ourselves to the best of our ability. The safety demonstration on aeroplanes echoes this lesson: Always put your own oxygen mask on first, before helping others.

A pebble in your shoe doesn't necessarily imply an absolute obstacle for close connection. Compared to an emergency situation on an aircraft, our social interactions are far more complex and can't be handled with a set of rules, such as 'I must always tend to my own needs first.' However, if we connect with our core and welcome our feelings, including the uncomfortable ones, it becomes easier to balance ourselves in the moment. We can attune ourselves to learn when we need to act and 'remove the pebble' or when we need to accept and 'embrace the pain from the pebble and invite it into the meeting'.

Look through your needs-coloured glasses

Based on the reasoning above, we suggest that you, other than micro-pausing, also make a habit out of putting on your 'needs-coloured glasses' when spending time with others – especially if you feel there's something bothering you or that just isn't quite right. You may feel angry or sad, or notice that something is making it hard for you to focus. In that case, direct your attention inward for a moment. Is there something upsetting you right now? Do you have any unmet needs? Is there something in your surroundings annoying you? Something you're feeling or thinking about, that would be good to bring out into the open? By 'checking in' like this, you can become aware of things like 'I need to change positions' or 'It feels so frustrating when he doesn't listen to me.' When you become aware of your own needs, you can also express them to your surroundings, which can make it easier to meet those needs.

Reflection exercise: Needs you often neglect with friends

Purpose: To identify needs that you sometimes or often neglect when you're with friends, and how to satisfy those needs.
Time required: 10–30 minutes
Method: Writing

How can you meet your own needs in social contexts? This exercise can help you identify what needs you usually have, what usually happens when you neglect them, and what you can do to actually meet your own needs.

1. *Go through your memory and pick out a difficult social situation.*
   Reflect on your past and imagine yourself back in a social situation that caused difficult feelings.

2. *Write down your unfulfilled needs.*
   Think about which unfulfilled needs may have caused the difficult feelings in this situation. Write down what comes to mind. If needed, use the table below for inspiration.

Security	Respect	Fun & play	Contact	Solidarity
Acceptance	Nourishment	Reciprocity	Touch	Intimacy
Justice	Simplicity	Autonomy	Clarity	Support
Sleep	Inspiration	Sympathy	Understanding	Communication
Trust	Movement	Participation	Predictability	Being seen
Calm	Integrity	Freedom of choice	Consideration	Freedom
Creativity	Honesty	Community	Effectivity	Acknowledgement
Cooperation	Rest	Validity	Order	Appreciation

3. *Draw a chart.*
   a) *Make a list of your unfulfilled needs.*
      After having analysed a specific situation, you can now write down which needs you generally tend to neglect. Answer the question: 'What needs do I have in social situations that I don't tend to care about as much as I would like?' Write down a few of those needs in the left column, as illustrated in the following chart.
   b) *Write down how you feel.*
      In the next column (the middle one), write down the emotional consequences of neglecting these needs.

c) *Write down potential solutions.*

In the right, third column, answer the question: 'What can I do to get what I need?'

Example chart with needs, emotional consequences, and potential solutions

Neglected needs	How do I feel when I neglect these needs	What can I do?
Rest, recuperation, sleep	*Tired and secluded *Frustrated *Drained of energy	*Tell others that I need to rest *Ask to come later *Suggest resting together
Being seen, being acknowledged	*Sad and low *Full of shame *Passive aggressive	*Express my feelings – that I feel excluded *Take up more space *Find other company
Belonging	*Sad *Jealous *Lonely	*Suggest an activity where everyone is included *Ask to join/participate *Steer the conversation towards topics we have in common
Inspiration	*Bored *Restless *Easily distracted	*Talk about something that interests me *Suggest an activity that engages me *Ask questions out of my curiosity
Security	*Insecure *Tense *Reserved	*Ask for more information *Ask for support *Tell others that I feel insecure because of X

Many of us aren't used to identifying which unfulfilled need is causing difficult emotions. Therefore, this exercise can be perceived as difficult. In Chapter 9, *Transforming conflicts*, you will get several tips and ideas about how you can express your wants and needs in a constructive way.

Thought problem or actual problem?

There is, of course, more than just unfulfilled needs which can prevent us from being present and responsive. It's also harder for us to become aware of our own core, as well as others', when too much of our attention is occupied by *thinking*. If we believe everything we think, there is a higher risk that we will do things that we don't actually want (such as dismiss compliments when we believe thoughts like: 'They're just saying that to be nice') and *not* do things that we actually want (such as telling a friend how much they mean to us when we believe thoughts like: 'It would sound insincere').

Imagine the following scenario: Lisa and Paul are having a cup of coffee together and Lisa is in a great mood. She is struck by how many exciting things Paul has to say and by how much she looks up to him. However, her self-criticism soon sets in. The thought 'He probably thinks I'm boring' runs through her mind and she quickly becomes gloomy. She tries to think of something to sound more interesting, but the effort unfortunately backfires – she becomes increasingly consumed by thinking about what she can say, rather than being present in the conversation. And as a result, she becomes incredibly self-conscious. What was Lisa's challenge in this situation? Was it that she *was* uninteresting, or that she *thought* that she was uninteresting? Or was the bigger issue that she started to engage too much in her thoughts, and listened more to them than she did to Paul?

Many of the problems that people struggle with can, when scrutinised carefully, prove to actually be *thought problems*, meaning problems which only originate from our own heads, and that cease to exist the very moment we stop indulging them. They can *develop* into actual problems if we focus a lot on the thoughts, or allow them to divert our attention and actions from the things we want and need. However, the risk tends to decrease if we understand the nature of thoughts; see them for what they are, and understand that we can choose how much to care about them.

Imagine that Lisa was posed the question: *If you could press a button to stop the thought that you are boring, how much of the difficulty you're experiencing would remain?* If you're struggling with thought problems like this, try asking yourself a similar question.

When thoughts call, you don't have to answer

We can't help that negative thoughts spontaneously pop into our head. We can't control them any more than we can control our heartbeats. However, we can control our *continued* thought process. As a metaphor, the brain can be compared to a phone that can't be put in silent mode: You can't choose whether or not it's going to ring, but you can choose if you're going to pick up or not. You can't control which thoughts 'ring' inside of you, but you can choose how much you *engage* with them. After all, you're the one who gets to decide how important a thought is allowed to be and, in many cases, that decision will become more important to your life and relationships than the actual thought that involuntarily emerged.

You may be better off ignoring some thoughts, in favour of the connection between you and your friend. Another way to free yourself from thoughts that prevent connection with others is to simply discuss them. Charged thoughts tend to discharge when brought out into the open. For instance, you may say 'I just had a thought that what I just said sounded childish.' Your friend may surprise you with their answer 'Oh! I was just thinking about how wise I think you are.'

Follow what sparks your interest

Imagine you're at a party and start chatting with someone you ended up next to. Your conversation partner awkwardly drones on about his hardware problems at work, and pretty quickly you notice that your interest fades. Nevertheless, you keep asking questions with a polite smile. Your forced enthusiasm keeps the conversation afloat for a good while, but your lack of genuine interest shines through your polite facade. Your conversation partner becomes insecure but keeps droning on.

Making small talk and being polite doesn't necessarily oppose achieving a deeper connection with someone – it can, of course, be a starting point for both people to open up and get to know each other. What can be problematic is if we become stuck on the surface level, while longing for deeper and more genuine interactions. Here, the habit of micropausing can be helpful. It can make it easier to connect with what's present in yourself. If you then have the courage to follow the impulse and steer towards what entices and attracts you, you can bring more energy into the conversation. You can stop and ask yourself what 'sparks your interest or turns you off'. If something turns you off, you may want to steer the conversation in a different direction or ask yourself if there is *anything* that sparks your interest. In the example above, a brief 'check in' like this could result in either you leaving the uninteresting conversation, *or* that you stop and ask him something that feels more interesting to you, such as: 'Hey, I'm curious – what made you apply for this job? To me, computers are boring.'

Other ways to get in touch with your curiosity – and others' – can be to shake up the typical forms of conversation. For instance, you can suggest a simple game where you take turns asking three questions each, or why not ask some of the thirty-six relation-building questions from the psychology researcher Arthur Aron, whom we mentioned earlier (see Appendix 1). Many of the games and exercises suggested in the next chapter serve such a purpose. But you can get far just by asking questions out of genuine curiosity. Authentic expressions usually fuel social interaction and lead to new ideas for conversation topics.

Does your way of expressing yourself serve your deeper wishes?

Most of us rarely think about why or how we talk. Usually, it just flows naturally, like a dance and, depending on who we meet, the dance expressions are a little different. We don't need an agenda or a plan. One upside of this is that it generally feels better to dance when we're not thinking about *how* we're dancing. A disadvantage can be that we keep dancing the same old dances over and over again.

Imagine the following scenario: Paul starts a new job and wants to develop a stronger bond to his new colleagues by being a little more open and personal. However, he tends to get stuck in his familiar role of joking around and, since that gets him a lot of appreciation, it's easy for him to just continue. But how will he become less reserved? Something that Paul could explore is micropausing during (or right before) a conversation and asking himself: 'Does my way of expressing myself serve what I really want?'

Why do you open your mouth? For instance, when you're on a coffee break and tell your colleagues in detail about a movie you just saw ... is it out of consideration for your listeners? Are you looking for attention and acknowledgement? Are you talking to avoid an awkward silence? Do you want to open up to a deeper connection with others? Are you using others as a kind of sketch pad to clarify your own thinking?

Sometimes, we feel like exploring and just playing intellectual tennis with someone else. Such conversations can also be engaging and relationship-developing. But regardless of the underlying incentive and specific conversation topic, we would like to encourage you to, during a conversation, briefly reflect on *what you want* from your conversation. If you do that, there is an increased probability that what you say will be aligned with your core. In turn, this lays the foundation for meetings with more connection.

In summary

To the same extent that you are in tune with your core – what you feel, need and want here and now – you enable others to connect with you. When we lose touch with our core, our social interactions are limited to more shallow levels. This can, for example, happen when we suppress parts of ourselves that we believe to be inappropriate or that feel uncomfortable. By regularly checking in on our inner state, for example by micropausing or slowing down, we can embrace and express more aspects of ourselves, become more present with others and improve our chances of finding connection.

CHAPTER 6
Entering your friend's world

It's 1:20 pm and you've been waiting for your friend Noah for over 15 minutes. When you check your phone for the fifth time without having heard from him, you start to feel uneasy. You remember how he seemed to have been offended by something you said the last time you saw each other, and the thought crosses your mind that this could be his way of punishing you. 'How typical of Noah,' you think. The more irritated you become, the harsher your inner accusations towards him become. Your feelings feed your hunt for evidence that confirms your thoughts, and you come up with several examples that all attest to Noah being an immature and unreliable person. You decide to give him a call and ask why he didn't show up. Noah answers: 'But we said that we'd meet at 2 pm, right?'

In the previous chapter we described how we can become more aware of our own feelings, needs and desires in the moment (what we refer to as connecting with our core). But in order for a sincere connection to occur, it isn't enough to just be in touch with what's present in ourselves. Therefore, in this chapter we will look deeper into how we can become more aware and responsive to what's present in our friends.

Interpretation or fact?

When someone does something that annoys us, we often think that it's because of their *personality*, but if we ourselves do the same thing, we're more inclined to explain it as being based on our *circumstances*. This is a well-known phenomenon called *the fundamental attribution error*. In the example above, with Noah, you could have believed that there were circumstances causing him to not show up on time or contact you. However, we're often more inclined to declare that someone *is* something: 'Noah is the type of person that doesn't respect agreements.'

There is a mantra that can help us deal with this 'programming malfunction'. We borrow this concept from Björn Natthiko Lindeblad, an author and former Buddhist monk. Allegedly, it was presented during a special evening when villagers and monks gathered by a monastery to find out the magical mantra that was said to be able to solve most of our problems. It stated: 'I could be wrong, I could be wrong, I could be wrong.' The mantra calls for humility. We don't have all the facts and we all make misjudgements, especially regarding how others think and feel.

In their book *Together*, psychologist Anna Kåver and psychiatrist Åsa Nilsonne use the metaphor that every person is an optical prism that breaks the light into a number of different colours. From them, we have minted the concept of 'Turning the prism', which we invite you to explore in the following exercise.

Reflection exercise: Turn the prism

Purpose: To illustrate how our perception of others is just one out of several possible perspectives
Time required: 3–5 minutes
Method: Mentally

In bad light

1. *Think of a friend.*

   Pick a friend, preferably one that you have mixed feelings about.
2. *Think back on a few situations when this friend has acted in a certain way that has affected you negatively.*

   Have they said or done things that have annoyed or hurt you? Try to bring forward this friend's *worst* traits and characteristics.
3. *Pay attention to how these memories affect your emotional mood.*

   While thinking about all these bad sides of your friend, notice how your body feels.

4. *Imagine how you would respond to this friend.*
   Now suppose that you were to meet your friend – what do you want to say and do? Can you imagine your body language?

In good light

5. *Keep thinking about the same friend.*
6. *Think back on situations when this friend has acted in a certain way that has affected you positively.*
   Have you felt appreciated or amused? Have you felt proud of your friend or happy for them? Try to remember your friend's *best traits* and characteristics.
7. *Pay attention to how these memories affect your emotional mood.*
   While thinking about all these good sides of your friend – notice how your body feels.
8. *Imagine how you would want to respond to this friend.*
   Suppose that you meet your friend again – what do you want to say and do? What is your body language like?

It was the same friend, but your feelings in the first and second part of the exercise were presumably different. If this friend had surprised you while you were doing this exercise, your way of greeting them and your tone of voice would likely be different, depending on which part of the exercise you were in. What we pay attention to, and focus on, in others matters.

We often notice things that match the perception we already have of someone. But if we turn the prism, more colours emerge, and we realise that what we perceived wasn't the full story. This can make us more *humble* and *curious*. What do you think would happen if you turned the prism while actually spending time with your friend?

If we try to fit people into our beliefs, we will never find their essence. As long as we love our images, we will never savour the surprise of meeting the person behind them.

(From the book *The Lies We Tell Ourselves*, by Jon Frederickson)

Let curiosity guide the way

In Zen-Buddhism there is an expression that says: 'Not knowing is the most intimate.' The most intimate interactions arise when we start off from a non-knowing position and let go of our preconceptions a little. This makes it easier for us to connect with our curiosity.

Petra, a friend of one of the authors, is known amongst her friends for being extra curious. She talks to strangers every day and is a master at establishing quick and positive connections. Petra says that she usually decides to be a little naive, like a child. She assumes that she doesn't know or understand and that raises a lot of questions. 'Most people have something interesting to say, and I can often learn something about myself when I gain insight into how others function. I usually ask myself what I really want to know, and then I ask about that. Then I usually don't settle for one answer, so I ask a lot of follow-up questions to really try to fully understand the other person's experience and perspective. Sometimes I can be a little brave and ask about sensitive subjects, but that demands a lot of intuition and sensitivity. I have to be observant of the other person's boundaries and take a step back if I notice that I'm crossing them.'

Playing games can also be a good way of keeping your curiosity going. Here are a few simple games that don't require any material or preparation. They can be played in all kinds of contexts – between two friends, during a walk, around a dinner table or at a party.

Connection game: The curiosity game[3]

Purpose: To stimulate curiosity and establish connection
Time required: 10–60 minutes
Method: Verbally with one or several friends

Read the instructions before you get started.
   1. *Choose a person (A) who gets to start receiving questions.*
   2. *Time to ask questions.*
      The others now get to ask person A questions (as many as they

---

3   The curiosity game is described in the *Authentic Relating Games Manual*, 2020, by Authentic Revolution.

want) out of pure curiosity, until they feel satisfied or during a certain amount of time (for example 5 minutes). Person A should *not answer* any of the questions.

3. *Person A gives feedback about the questions.*

When the people asking the questions feel satisfied or when the set time is up, it's person A's turn to talk. They then say which questions were the most engaging to them personally, which thoughts and feelings were stirred, and possibly why some questions felt less engaging. For example: 'The question about my relationship with my mother interested me the most. It brought out feelings of both love and sorrow, because I was reminded about how much I care about her and that I don't always manage to convey those feelings.' Person A doesn't need to remember all the questions, just remember what they remember (which is usually the questions that touched them the most).

4. *Person A answers the questions they want.*

If A would like, they can later answer one or several of the questions, but they don't *have* to answer a single question. Here, you can also agree on a certain time limit, or let A talk until the question-askers indicate that they are satisfied, by saying 'thank you'.

5. *Switch roles.*

If you're just two people playing, you now switch roles. If there are several people, you choose a new person and start over from step 2 until everyone has had a chance to be 'person A', or until you feel ready to end the game.

One advantage of this game is that it can feel liberating to be allowed to ask questions without having to think about whether or not the person receiving them wants to answer. Our genuine curiosity can take up more space when we don't have to limit ourselves to what we think others would or would not like to share.

Furthermore, there is a good chance that the receiver of the questions feels seen and appreciated when they receive the interest of others. Another bonus is that the questions that aren't answered during the actual game can serve as seeds for new conversations at other times.

Connection game: The Google game[4]

Purpose: To stimulate curiosity and establish connection
Time required: 2–20 minutes
Method: Verbally with at least one friend

Like the curiosity game above, this game doesn't require any preparation. It's easy-going and can be played in several different contexts – perhaps during a family reunion or on a date. Start off by reading the instructions.

1. *Agree on a time limit.*

   Decide how long each person should be 'Googled' (for example 5–10 minutes).

2. *Choose a person to begin being Googled (person A).*

3. *Someone starts to Google person A.*

   The people that are Googling start off by thinking about what they feel like Googling about A. They ask questions or decide on a few key words just as they would write them when actually Googling something on their computer. For example: 'I'm Googling you and *your fears* – what hits do I get?' or 'What hits do I get if I google *your deepest desires?*'

4. *The person being Googled answers.*

   They can either say 'Access denied' (if they don't want to talk about that specific subject) or they can share which hits pop up. 'Hits' refers to spontaneous thoughts, memories or associations of the subject (hence, person A should not answer what the actual hits on the internet would be). For example, person A being Googled on *love* could talk about their relationship with their partner as it is in the moment or how it used to be.

5. *Anyone can click on 'internet links'.*

   If the others are curious about something that person A has said, they can say that they 'click' on what they want to hear more about, for example 'I click on *relationship getting better and better.*' Person A can still say 'access denied', or choose to go deeper into the subject or the search word.

---

4   The Google game comes from Amy Silverman and The Connection Movement (NY).

6. *Anyone can interrupt A and keep Googling other topics.*
   If the people Googling lose interest or feel that they have gotten enough answers, they can interrupt, say thank you, and keep searching for other things, even if A is in the middle of a story. The interest of the person Googling leads the search, just like when actually Googling something on your computer.

7. *Switch roles.*
   When the time is up or when you feel content, you switch roles and start again from step 2. Now person A gets to start Googling someone else.

Ask open-ended questions and get richer answers

Imagine that you are playing a murder-mystery game – someone named John has been found dead next to a puddle of water. Other than that, the only thing you are told is that the person who last saw John is named Bob. Now you get the opportunity to talk to Lina, who witnessed the course of events. You get to ask her questions to try to figure out what happened, *but* you can only use so-called *closed questions* (i.e., yes or no questions). How would your conversation sound?

> You: *'Was a weapon used?'*
> Lina: *'No.'*
> You: *'Was Bob mad at John?'*
> Lina: *'No.'*
> You: *'Was John mad at Bob?'*
> Lina: *'No.'*
> You: *'Did John slip?'*
> Lina: *'Nooo.'*

After a while, Lina gets tired and reveals that Bob is a cat and John is a goldfish.

The questions we ask impact the kind of answers we get, and there are things that we may *never* get to know if we only ever ask closed questions. Our questions also say something about what we are ready to take in. What do you want to answer if someone asks you 'Everything good with you?' compared to 'How are you doing?' Or: 'Did you have fun this weekend?' as opposed to 'How was your weekend?' There's nothing wrong with closed questions, but *open-ended questions* — the kinds that don't have any given options as answers – can lead us into unknown territory that we didn't know existed.

As our curiosity-expert friend Petra so wisely said, you can get to know someone a lot better by not settling for just *one* answer. When your friend says that she's upset with her partner you may think 'I understand completely', but are you certain? Can you ask further questions to deepen your understanding? Questions like: 'What do you think about that?', 'How did that make you feel?' or 'Why did you do that?' can help you get even closer to your friend's experience.

Is there a friend (or family member or colleague) that you've stopped being curious about? Maybe someone you care about but think you already know everything about? If so, it can be helpful to actively try to reignite your curiosity about that person. What would you genuinely want to know about them? Write down some questions that you could ask. Maybe you'll notice that one question leads to another, and all of a sudden you have a whole lot of interesting ideas. The next time you see this person they may not be that uninteresting after all.

Listen to understand

Do you ever start preparing what you're going to say before the person you're talking to has finished speaking? You may think that you know what they're getting at halfway through their story, and feel yourself becoming increasingly restless to get to say what you want? Or perhaps you've had the experience of how it feels when a friend isn't really listening to you. They may just let you talk, waiting for their turn to speak their mind.

We can listen with different intentions. We often listen to *respond*. We take for granted that others want to hear about our thoughts and opinions, without knowing if that's actually the case. We then tend to focus on ourselves and on our own thoughts. We can also listen with the intention of *supporting*. A common mistake is to offer well-meant advice, without knowing if that's really what the other person wants or needs. The impulse to go into problem-solving mode can be extra strong if we ourselves have a hard time coping with feelings of discomfort. If a friend shares something that is difficult, it can be very easy for us to offer suggestions about how to solve the situation, which may only be serving to help ourselves to avoid uncomfortable feelings. This can result in us inadvertently sending signals to the other person that their feelings are wrong and need to be changed.

Yet another way of listening is listening to *understand*. Try to remember a situation when you perceived that the person you were with really wanted to understand you. How did it feel? What was it about that person's way of listening that made you feel they were interested? Presumably, that person wasn't focused on offering you advice, but on exploring, asking questions and trying to understand how you were thinking and feeling.

The authors Anna Kåver and Åsa Nilsonne (from whom we borrowed the prism-metaphor) illustrate it as each of us sitting in our own 'lookout-tower' with a certain, limited perspective. When we listen to understand, it can be compared to jumping over to someone else's lookout-tower for a moment, to see what their view is like from there. This is often referred to as active or empathetic listening, as we will describe below.

Control your attention

What kind of experience do you want to have with your friend, and is your focus aligned with what you find important there and then? If you're sitting with your uncle and listening to his boring fishing story for the billionth time, maybe you can allow your thoughts to wander off to other things for a while. The fact that you're spending time together may be more important than the actual conversation topic. But if you're with a friend that you want to become closer to and get to know better, it's probably more beneficial to focus on your conversation.

If we want to listen more intently, we have to make an *active* choice, repeatedly, to maintain our focus where we want it. This can be challenging, especially if our attention span is like an untrained puppy running after every ball. But, just as puppies with kind and patient owners can become obedient over time, so can your attention, if you kindly but firmly reel it in every time it slips away. You can also be open with the person you're talking to and admit that you lost your focus, and ask them to repeat themselves: 'I'm sorry, could you repeat that last part? I wasn't entirely with you.'

Our bodies can also be helpful in these situations. For instance, how we sit and which direction we are facing sends a clear message – both to the person we're talking to, and to ourselves – about how interested we are and what we want. When we decide to turn towards the friend we're with and look them in the eye, it's as if we're telling our brains and hearts that 'this is what's important right now'. This makes it easier to really take in what we see and hear.

Welcome silence

'Should I cut in and say something now, or wait and just continue to listen? Should I give in to the impulse to speak or should I resist it?' Choices like this arise all the time. Are you aware of them?

In some cultures, it's considered polite to be quiet for a while after someone has spoken before you speak. Replying too quickly is considered rude, since it shows that you haven't really taken the time to listen. In other cultures, the word exchange is so fast that you're *expected* to interrupt if you want to get a word in edgewise. Some people prefer when conversations are fast and full of rapid changes like this, since the high intensity can contribute to a feeling of a relaxed and open-minded environment. However, if we want to listen to *understand*, it's often wise to slow down the pace and make room for pauses. A slower pace allows us to notice things that would otherwise just flicker by. We give ourselves – and perhaps our conversation partner as well – time to take in, feel and digest what is being said.

Connection game: The walkie-talkie game

Purpose: To feel the peace that arises when you're allowed to speak without being interrupted, and to become aware of the balance between how much you talk and how much space you offer others
Time required: Can be played for a short or long period of time
Method: In conversation with at least one friend

The idea of this game came to the authors while on the phone with bad network coverage. The sound was delayed in a way that caused our voices to repeatedly collide. To be able to have a conversation, we agreed to simply take turns talking and listening. Other times, when we've met face-to-face, we've tried to do the same thing, without blaming the bad connection. The result has been the same as over the phone: the person talking feels more at ease, knowing that they can take their time and finish speaking, and taking turns makes it easier for everyone to listen intently. This game can be particularly rewarding for those who tend to be eager to speak and often interrupt others.

1. *Agree on a time frame.*
   For example, set aside 10 minutes for this game. You can talk about anything you want (for instance, keep talking about what you were discussing before one of you suggested this game).

2. *Take turns talking.*
   When one person (A) speaks, the other (B) is silent. B can nod, hum or express themselves non-verbally, but they *cannot* say anything. When A feels satisfied, they say (just like with a walkie-talkie) 'Over', and then B can begin to speak. Continue switching between talking and listening until the time is up, or for as long as you both think it feels meaningful.

3. *Share your thoughts and feelings.*
   End the game by talking about how you experienced it, and how it felt to talk and listen in turns.

Needless to say, switching between talking and listening in such a rigid way isn't very natural. But hopefully it can be a playful way for you to become more aware of, and maybe even start to talk about, *how* you talk to each other.

Listen beyond the words

When someone asks how you're doing, it's easy to just say 'Good, thanks!' even though you're actually feeling something completely different. It's harder to lie with your body language. Your tone of voice, facial expressions and posture aren't as easy to manipulate. In the 1960s, the American anthropologist Ray Birdwhistell suggested that only 30 per cent of the information conveyed in a conversation consists of what is actually said. The exact percentage can be discussed, but there is no question that a large part of our communication is expressed without words. Therefore, it's no coincidence that it's easier to misunderstand each other when communicating through writing.

A simplified way of describing different levels of listening is to distinguish between listening *superficially* and listening *deeply*. Often, we listen superficially, meaning that we listen to *what* is being said. When we listen deeply, we're trying to refine our understanding of the other person's feelings, needs and desires (their 'core'). We're interested in both *what* is being said and *how* it is being expressed. If your colleague complains to you about a client who acted like a stubborn five-year-old, a superficial listening would mean that you stick with the description of the immature client. Perhaps you agree, or you question it. But deep listening requires that you, other than listening to the description of the client, also interpret your colleague's tired body language and low tone of voice. This type of listening makes it easier for you to get a sense of their feelings and needs, whereupon you for example could ask: 'Are you worn out? Should we take a coffee break?'

Since it can be easy to misunderstand the unspoken, it's a good idea to every now and then reflect back what you've perceived, to see how accurate your interpretation is. 'I noticed that you seemed a little gloomy when you came to work today, but I get the feeling that you don't want to talk about it . . . am I right?'

Reflect to comprehend

Repeating what you have perceived is often referred to as reflecting. The most simple form of reflecting is to literally repeat word-for-word some of what you've heard. Your friend complains: 'I get so damn frustrated that nobody cares about this!' and you reply with a simple: 'You get really frustrated.' A more complex way of reflecting would be to repeat something *other than* what was verbally expressed. Maybe you sensed an underlying meaning or feeling.

When you reflect back to the other person, you give yourself some time to contemplate what you've heard. Reflecting is also a clear indication that you're really listening and that you're interested in your friend, which can help them to open up even more. Reflecting can also be a good way for you to fine-tune your understanding. By reflecting what you heard and perceived, you give the other person the opportunity to correct any misconceptions.

A: 'I hear that you don't want Tim to spend time with Greg any more. Are you feeling jealous?'
B: 'No, not at all! I understand why you might think that, but that's actually the last thing I want. I was just hoping that he would understand why I reacted so strongly last Tuesday.'

Since there's always a possibility that our perceptions are *incorrect*, it's important that we're clear about them just being interpretations and guesses, not definite truths. If you, for example, say: 'I notice that you light up when you talk about this, it really seems to make you happy! Would you agree?' the other person has the chance to agree or dismiss your interpretation: 'No, I guess I'm smiling because I'm touched.'

Sometimes, our mouth and our body seem to contradict each other. If you ask your friend how they're doing and they say, 'I'm fine', but their hunched posture and dull facial expressions display sadness, try to reflect your interpretation to see if it's accurate. Besides getting a better understanding of what's going on, it can help your friend get a better insight into themself.

Portable tool: Listen deeply

Purpose: To deepen your understanding of what is the most relevant to the person you're spending time with, while you're together
Time required: 1–30 seconds
Method: In conversation with a friend

This tool summarises deep listening, and can be used when talking to a friend with whom you would like to become closer.

1. *Remind yourself of your wish to become closer to the other person.*
   Let this intention set the tone for the following moments.
2. *Anchor yourself in presence.*
   Slow down for a moment: Feel your body from the inside and out, let go of your own imagination and thoughts, and make yourself fully accessible to the other person.
3. *Pay attention to what seems important to the other person.*
   Listen to both *what* is being said and *how* it's said. What is the other person feeling? What seems to be most important in this moment?
4. *Ensure that you're interpreting the other person accurately.*
   Every now and then, check to see that you've understood by reflecting and posing follow-up questions such as: 'Do you mean that . . . ', 'I'm hearing that . . . ', and 'It sounds like the most important thing to you is . . . '

In summary

We often listen to respond instead of listening to understand. With curiosity, games, open-ended questions and deep listening, the probability increases that we can bring forward what is most important to our friends. A clear perception of the other person's core lays a solid foundation for deeper connection and a stronger friendship.

CHAPTER 7
Vulnerable and reachable

It's Saturday morning. Thomas texts his friend John to ask if they should start the weekend with a work-out together. After a while, John finally replies that he's too tired.

A few days later Thomas meets his colleague Hannah for lunch. She says in passing 'Your friend John is so nice.' A few seconds pass before Thomas reacts. 'Ah, you know him?' he asks. She replies 'Yes, I thought he told you. We met at your party, and later on he contacted me. We took a long walk together last Saturday. It was really nice!'

After work Thomas calls John: 'Hey, what's up? Feeling better? Did you get any rest this weekend?' 'Yeah . . . ' John replies, hesitating. Thomas tells John he knows he and Hannah spent Saturday together and awaits an answer, but John is silent. 'Are you hitting on Hannah?' Thomas asks. John replies 'Um, I should have told you, but yeah, I'm interested in her.'

Thomas is surprised to realise that his close friend was trying to hide a date with the woman he himself had had a crush on for months. For a split second, Thomas hesitates. Should he ignore it? Or be honest and tell John how hurt he feels, with the risk of conflict? Thomas merely mumbles 'OK, well, good for you', and then changes the subject.

Close connection is promoted by opening the door to our core by showing and expressing what we feel, need and want. Since there are no guarantees that we will be met in a loving way when doing so, it takes courage – courage to be vulnerable. Brené Brown, researcher and vulnerability expert, describes being vulnerable as 'uncertainty, risk and emotional exposure'. In this chapter we will take a closer look at what it means and what can stand in its way.

Risks and benefits when being vulnerable

In the example above, Thomas would probably have felt more vulnerable if he, instead of putting a lid on it, had said something like: 'Well, I'm happy for you, John, but it also makes me sad and angry, because you *know* that I've had feelings for Hannah for a long time. I really wish you would've said something.' John could have dismissed him as grudging and jealous. Or – even worse – he could have told Hannah, and Thomas could have been rejected by both of them. Why would Thomas want to take that risk?

The word vulnerable means *being able to be hurt*. Considering our mortality, our *physical* vulnerability is considered to be innate and inevitable. But when it comes to relationships, our *emotional* vulnerability is more interesting. Is that inevitable as well? Or is it more of a choice? At least in theory, we can reduce the risk of being emotionally hurt by building a metaphorical wall between ourselves and others. But how meaningful is life behind armoured walls?

The Swedish poet Karin Boye wrote the following passage in her collection of poems *Hidden Lands*: 'You shall thank your Gods when your shell they break, reality and essence, the sole choice you can make.' Sometimes we are forced to tear down our walls and expose our inner essence, to ourselves and to others. But we can also *choose* to be vulnerable. We can voluntarily take the risk of being emotionally exposed.

When self-help coaches advocate vulnerability, you can get the impression that the more vulnerable we can be, the better. But in some situations, it's inappropriate to expose yourself. If someone has deliberately hurt you and you have good reason to believe that it will happen again, it's probably wise to maintain your shield or avoid that person altogether. And in certain situations, for example in professional contexts, where the primary purpose isn't to establish emotionally close connections, it's also inappropriate to be completely open about how you feel. But if you think about mutual relationships that you hope to deepen, does the situation change?

Giving others a chance to see you

'What we hunger for perhaps more than anything else, is to be seen in our full humanness, and yet that is often what we fear more than anything else.'

These words come from the author Frederick Buechner's autobiography, *Telling Secrets*. When you open up to someone, it's like taking a leap into the unknown, and that can feel scary. But at the same time, it makes you accessible and 'reachable'. When you expose the sides of yourself that you often withhold from others, your 'ugly', 'weak' and 'embarrassing' sides, you give them a chance to see and accept all of you, and say 'You're OK', 'I want to be here with you even though you're feeling down', or ' . . . even though you're acting a little childish.' 'Sure, I think you look a little silly when you burst into your unrestrained laughter, but I love that you have the guts to laugh so freely' or 'I like you, because you can lower your guard and be natural, and because you help me to do the same.' This makes it possible to meet and connect completely and utterly. Exposing your core like this, and choosing to be vulnerable, is therefore the first step to sincere connection with others.

Reflection exercise: A taste of vulnerability[5]

Purpose: To become aware of deeper layers of yourself that can be sensitive to talk about
Time required: 5–10 minutes
Method: Writing, alone or with a friend

---

5 Adapted from the 'non dominant hand exercise' in *A Guide to Functional Analytic Psychotherapy: Awareness, Courage, Love and Behaviorism*, by M. Tsai, R. J. Kohlenberg, J. Kanter, B. Kohlenberg, W. Follette & G. Callaghan, New York: Springer, 2009.

This writing exercise, to be done with your non-dominant hand, comes from our colleagues that developed the therapy method mentioned earlier – FAP, functional analytic psychotherapy. They suggest that a right-handed person that writes with their left hand often writes more unfiltered. Of course, the same applies to a left-handed person writing with their right hand. You can do this exercise alone, but it can also be good to do with one or several friends.

1. *Finish the sentences.*

   Get a pen and a piece of paper and finish the following sentences with your non-dominant hand. Don't think too much, just try to write what spontaneously comes to mind. If you can't find an answer, move on to the next sentence.

   I feel . . .
   I dream of . . .
   I'm struggling with . . .
   I pretend that I . . .
   If I had the courage, I would . . .
   Something I rarely share with others is that . . .
   I'm afraid of . . .
   I'm longing for . . .

2. *Notice how you feel.*

   How did it feel to write these sentences? And if you read them – how does it feel? Does any particular sentence make you feel particularly vulnerable?

3. *Share with each other.*

   If you're doing this exercise with one or several friends, you can now read all or some of what you've written aloud to each other.

If you were surprised by something that popped up during this exercise, you may want to give yourself some extra time to let it sink in. Perhaps you'll get a new insight or hint about something that's important to you – maybe something you're longing for but have overlooked or disregarded, or something you feel and want to express.

Vulnerability in large and small matters

Vulnerability isn't limited to big life crises or great losses. We don't need to put ourselves on display in front of thousands of people on social media in order to feel vulnerable – the feeling can emerge even in the most common situations of our everyday life. For most of us, it's enough to just say hi to a new person at a party, give our partner a hug after an argument, or ask a friend to do us a favour. When we asked our friends about what can make them feel vulnerable we got lots of different answers:

> When I sing or dance in front of others.
> When I show someone my messy home.
> When I go out without having done my hair and make-up.
> When I get nervous and don't try to hide it.
> When I say hi to someone new at a party.
> When I hang out with someone even though I'm feeling tired and pitiful.
> When I'm open about not getting the point of a joke.
> When I share something that I've failed at.
> When I admit that I've lied or exaggerated to get acknowledgement.
> When I apologise for saying or doing something stupid.
> When I've cooked for others and I don't think that the meal was very good.
> When I share that I feel uncertain about my self-worth.
> When I show that my feelings were hurt by what somebody said.
> When I ask for help.
> When I decline an invitation to get together.
> When I take the initiative to get together without knowing if the other person wants to hang out with me.
> When I say, 'I like you.'
> When I maintain eye contact with someone for a longer period of time.

Can you relate to any of the examples above? In the next exercise, contemplate when you tend to feel vulnerable.

Reflection exercise: When do you feel vulnerable?

Purpose: To increase your awareness of what feels vulnerable to you
Time required: 5–15 minutes
Method: Writing

1. *Write down what makes you feel vulnerable.*

   Think about if you can relate to any of the examples above. Also, contemplate if there is something else that you do (or could do) in your relationship with friends that can make you feel vulnerable. It can be big or small things. Write down two to five things or situations.

2. *Write down risks.*

   For every example you've written down, think about and write down what *risks* you take (even if they're small) by doing these things. How could you be hurt? For example: 'By someone thinking that I'm boring and negative when I show my sadness' or 'By someone not answering or letting me join the conversation when I'm trying to get into a group of people.'

3. *Write down costs.*

   Now contemplate and write down what it costs you, or what it would cost you, to *not* take these risks. For example: 'It's exhausting to try to be happy and energetic when that's not always how I feel' or 'I feel more lonely.'

4. *Write down the gains.*

   Identify what the gains are, or could be, of *taking* these risks. For example: 'I could feel accepted for who I am' or 'I can participate and be a part of the group.'

If you think it could be valuable for you to be (more) open and vulnerable in your friendships, the following sequence will hopefully be helpful. We start off by looking at a typical obstacle and two common strategies to avoid feeling and being vulnerable.

Vulnerability and shame

Vulnerability means that we expose ourselves emotionally, and shame is one of the main reasons that we try to avoid it. Shame is a painful experience of 'being wrong'. It's a feeling that can be ignited when we have said or done something that we think could cause others to dislike or reject us. Shame is related to guilt, but the difference is that guilt is connected to what we *have done*, whereas shame is connected to who we *are*. While we tend to withdraw when feeling shame, we typically want to get closer to others and set things straight when feeling guilt, for example by apologising.

Shame usually passes quickly if, when telling others, we're met in a non-judgmental manner. And vice versa, conveying non-acceptance can be an effective way of increasing someone's feeling of shame. If we frequently experience shame, it often derives from something we learned as part of our culture or upbringing. If others have rolled their eyes and mocked us when we've been spontaneous, happy, sad or scared, it can develop over time into a belief that there is something fundamentally wrong with us. 'The shame started as something that two people participated in, but as I grew older, I learned to create feelings of shame on my own', a man shares in Brené Brown's book *Daring Greatly: How the Courage to Be Vulnerable Transforms the Way We Live, Love, Parent, and Lead*. We maintain a facade or put on a mask to survive in an environment where we have to hide our feelings and parts of ourselves in order to be accepted. We simply find it too risky to expose our true selves to the world. But with the mask on, we lose the opportunity of being authentic and intimate with others.

The organisation Authentic Relating Training International has come up with a model that illustrates different possible approaches to the feeling of shame. It describes how we can lose contact with others as well as with ourselves by *collapsing* and making ourselves smaller than we actually are, or by *posturing*, becoming pompous and making ourselves bigger. All to avoid exposing our own vulnerability. The model also illustrates how we can open up to connect with others by finding the way back to our *dignity* and our *humility*. It is between this range that we find our vulnerability. Here is a revised version of the model.

Balance

POSTURING (BLAME)	DIGNITY	HUMILITY	COLLAPSING (SHAME)

Closed to connection   Open to connection   Closed to connection

Dignity and humility

When we are open to connection we are in balance between humility and dignity. We are in the middle zones of the model. Within the *dignified* spectrum, we feel worthy – that our voice is important, our thoughts and opinions are relevant, and that we have something to offer. We own our truth and stand up for it (think of Nelson Mandela). Within the *humble* range, we realise that the people in our surroundings have experiences and knowledge that we ourselves lack, and that we can learn from them. We're genuinely interested in others' perspectives and realise that everyone, big or small, brings something to the table (think Mother Teresa). When we are in balance between humility and dignity, we can contribute with our own wisdom, while also being open to learning from the people in our surroundings. It's as if the floodgate is open in both directions – we can both give and take in the meeting with others. Therefore, the middle zone, between dignity and humility, is where we are the most accessible to a connection with others.

Posturing

On the left side of the model, we move past the dignity zone in the model above into posturing. We do this to avoid exposing ourselves and risk feeling shame. We think that we're better and know more than everyone else, with a disregard to the valuable perspectives of others. We may speak negatively of someone who isn't present, look for faults in others, or set unreasonable expectations and demands on others. An example would be the image of a high school bully, who flexes his muscles to feel big and strong: 'I'm the best! If you don't agree, get lost!'

A more subtle version of the posturing is when we show others that we are flawless and self-sufficient. Perhaps we decorate a perfect home based on the latest trends of interior design, work out to get the perfect body or buy the most expensive coffee at the coolest café, just to shine and perform everything correctly. A characteristic thought is that we don't need others as much as they need us: 'I'm doing great! *You*, on the other hand, could use *my* help.'

Collapse

On the right side of the model, we move *past* the humility zone and collapse in shame. We can, quite literally, physically collapse, avoid eye contact, withdraw and make ourselves unreachable, like a turtle crawling into its shell. We diminish ourselves, perhaps from an unspoken idea that we're unworthy, through a focus on everything we haven't done right: 'I shouldn't think that I'm anything special.' In a state of collapse, we can feel numb, empty, and lonely as we've withdrawn from connection with others. Another, more subtle version of collapsing is that we simply avoid certain contexts or conversation topics to avoid exposing ourselves. For instance, we withhold private matters or hide parts of ourselves from even our closest friends and family (for example, not telling anyone that we have a serious illness or that we love to dance the tango).

Lastly, another version of collapsing can be to become a 'helper'. We become the shoulder who everyone wants to cry on but don't expect a shoulder to cry on in return. We adapt and adjust ourselves in an attempt to please others. In doing so, we neglect our own needs, as an overexaggerated focus on others keeps us from acknowledging that we have a will and a voice of our own.

Reflection exercise: Your favourite hideaways

Purpose: To become more aware of when and how you make yourself
inaccessible by being emotionally invulnerable
Time required: 5–15 minutes
Method: Writing

1. *Write down situations when you've ended up in (or gotten close to)
   one of the outer zones in the model.*
   Contemplate if you can relate to either posture or collapse.
   Perhaps there are certain relationships where you easily glide
   into one of them. Try to find and write down at least one specific
   situation where that has happened.
2. *Write down behaviours which make you emotionally invulnerable.*
   Think about what you *did* or *didn't do* in the situation. It can be
   hard, especially if the behaviours are subtle, but give it a try.
   Imagine seeing yourself in a surveillance video – what would
   you notice? For example, it could be that you refrained from
   saying something important, toned down how happy you
   were when you received acknowledgement, avoided eye contact, answered questions very briefly or lied about your plans
   for the weekend.
3. *Write down behaviours which make you vulnerable.*
   Think about what you would have done if instead you had
   remained in the middle zone, that is – in touch with both your
   dignity and your humility. It could be that you would've shared
   that you were worried about your mother, that you would
   have shown how happy you were, that you would have looked
   the other person in the eye or told the truth about your weekend plans.

Can you see where in the model you tend to end up? Most of us
alternate between being more or less dignified, humble, posturing and
collapsing depending on the context of the situation and who we're
with. We hope that this model and exercise can help you recognise
how *posture* and *collapse* manifest themselves in you. By simply

noticing that you approached or ended up in one of the outer zones, you've taken a step closer to the middle section, where the conditions are better for establishing sincere connection.

Showing vulnerability

How can we embrace our vulnerability instead of collapsing in shame or arrogantly posturing? How can we remain dignified and humble, so that we can see what is valuable in ourselves and others? These are questions that we will now take a closer look at.

Levels of vulnerability in conversation

A common obstacle to intimacy in our everyday lives is that we get stuck in trivialities. We talk about the weather and avoid more profound conversations, since it can feel risky to express who we are, what we believe, and what we think. Personal and vulnerable conversations are not necessarily 'better', but we can miss out on a lot if we never take the opportunity to also express more personal and intimate thoughts and feelings. If we notice that we, year after year, practically *only* talk about work-related technicalities with a friend we want to become closer to, it can be enriching to also explore deeper layers of intimacy. The opposite is more uncommon – that the conversations in a friendship only revolve around personal issues. Therefore, we generally benefit more from improving our ability to move towards more intimacy than the other way around.

The educational company Authentic Relating Training International has designed a model that illustrates three different levels of conversation. The purpose is to help us become aware of the different levels, so that we can navigate more easily between them in a flexible way. The three levels are:

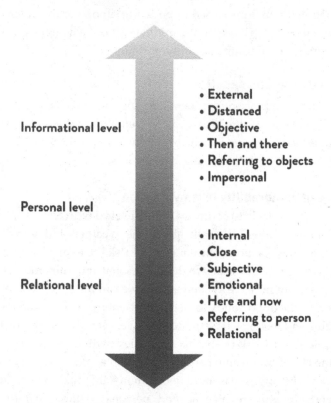

Informational level
- External
- Distanced
- Objective
- Then and there
- Referring to objects
- Impersonal

Personal level

Relational level
- Internal
- Close
- Subjective
- Emotional
- Here and now
- Referring to person
- Relational

Informational level

We speak in an impersonal way about external matters that have happened or will happen, and about things we've done or will do. We discuss ideas or theories, but don't reveal as much about ourselves. The informational level is in general the level that makes us feel the *least* vulnerable, since we talk about matters outside of ourselves. However, conversations on this level can be a good way of 'breaking the ice' and establishing a connection.

Examples: 'What did you do on your vacation?', 'I saw a movie yesterday, it was about . . . ', 'My kids think school is so fun', 'Could you recommend a good restaurant?', 'Did you see the game last Friday?'

Personal level

We show more of ourselves by sharing *our own experiences* and what we *feel* about events and people. We share what we care about, what's important to us, and our likes and dislikes. We reveal more about our values and our identity, matters that are close to our hearts.

Examples: 'I'm feeling pretty exhausted at work lately', 'It's going to be so wonderful to see my grandkids next weekend!', 'I've just started dating again, it feels pretty scary', 'The fires in the Amazon make me so sad and upset!'

Relational level

We pay attention to and talk about what is happening *between us* and how we are affected by each other. We share what we think and feel *in the moment* and are also interested in the other person's experience here and now. Perhaps we talk about how we feel about each other or shed light on something that's wearing at the relationship. This is the level that often feels the most exposed and vulnerable. If we navigate towards this level, we can within minutes experience that we get a deeper connection.

Examples: 'When you're silent and look away like that, I get so curious about what you're thinking', 'I notice that I always smile a lot when I'm with you!', 'I really appreciate that we can talk about so many things', 'I just had a thought that you might think that I'm bragging', 'How does it feel for you to talk about this?', 'What interesting conversation topics you bring up – talking to you is really stimulating.'

Connection game: Navigate between different levels of conversation

Purpose: To become aware of how the different levels of conversation affect the connection between you and your friend
Time required: Can be done during a shorter or longer period of time, but we suggest that you start off with 10 minutes
Method: In conversation with at least one friend

1. *Talk about anything.*
   Just continue on with the conversation as you were before one of you suggested this game.
2. *Notice and state the different levels of conversation.*
   While you're talking, notice what level you're on and hold up 1, 2 or 3 fingers to indicate (1= informational level, 2= personal level, and 3= relational level).
3. *Navigate up and down between the levels of conversation.*
   Alternate freely between the different levels, but make sure to try level 3 at least once. Use the list below to get ideas about how to get there.
4. *Reflect together.*
   When you've played this game for a while, talk about how you experienced the different levels and what happened with the connection between you when you switched between the levels.

Examples of sentences that can be used to initiate the navigation to the relational level (level 3):

Now that you say/ask X, I feel/think/get . . .
Now that I'm saying X, I feel/think/get . . .
Now that we're talking about this, I feel/think/get . . .
How do you feel now that you/I/we . . . ?
I imagine that you're feeling/thinking/getting . . . ?
Sitting here with you, I notice that . . .

Reveal what you feel

Are there feelings that you're reluctant to show with your facial expressions and your body language? What are you afraid that others will think or do if you show them? Emotional openness is an important ingredient in close relationships. However, we are sometimes careful about showing what we feel. We might have experiences of others becoming uncomfortable when we've shown our genuine joy. Or perhaps we've been met in a way that we really *didn't* need when we've shown our sadness. Add to that our culture, which often views negative feelings as a sign of failure.

Several studies indicate that sincere emotional expressions with our body and face contribute to increased closeness in relationships. Conversely, people who suppress their non-verbal emotional expressions tend to feel less support from, or closeness to, others, and less social satisfaction. Part of the explanation is that we can become stressed when someone's body language and facial expressions aren't congruent with their words or feelings. It becomes more difficult for us to understand them and their intentions. In other words, we have a lot to gain by daring to show our natural expressions of emotion.

Expose your joy

When we share something that we are happy about or proud of, we risk coming off as boastful and self-absorbed. We also risk making other people jealous. But when we expose our joy, we can also become closer to one another, something that often happens when we experience wellbeing together and share our joys.

Reflection exercise: Twenty things I'm proud of[6]

Purpose: To practise owning and sharing your dignity and worthiness
Time required: 5–20 minutes
Method: Writing, preferably with a friend

This exercise is borrowed from colleagues who developed the previously mentioned therapy, FAP. It's about highlighting things that we like about ourselves, which can make us feel vulnerable. It can make us doubtful, 'Is this really true?', and it can cause grief, if we notice that we find it difficult to think good things about ourselves. We can also be reminded of the opposite of what we're pleased with – things that we *don't* like about ourselves. If we also take the risk of *telling someone else* what we like about ourselves, we can feel even more vulnerable. On the other hand, it can be a way to invite the other person into our world and show that we trust them not to judge or hurt us.

---

6   Adapted from the exercise '100 positives' printed in the article 'Introduction to using structured evocative activities in Functional Analytic Psychotherapy', by K. M. Nelson, J. P. Yang, A. C. Maliken, M. Tsai & R. J. Kohlenberg, *Cognitive & Behavioral Practice*, 2014.

To increase the intensity of this exercise, you can do it with a friend, even if it's also enriching to do it on your own. Make sure to set aside enough time, or do one section at a time.

1. *Make a list of what you're proud of.*
   Get a pen and a piece of paper and write down between ten and forty things that you like about yourself. It can be your character-istics, accomplishments, talents, or your physical appearance, for example: Good at acknowledging others, thoughtful, empathetic, in good shape, pretty eyes, and so on. If you're doing the exercise with a friend, you each write a list.
2. *Share with a friend.*
   If you're doing the exercise with a friend, read your lists to each other. Preferably, formulate full sentences that begin with 'I', for example: 'I'm good at acknowledging others', 'I'm empathetic', and so on. If you're doing the exercise on your own, read the list aloud to yourself.
3. *Add to the lists.*
   If you want, you can now add things to each other's lists – things that you appreciate and that haven't already been mentioned. If you're doing the exercise on your own, we suggest that you think about what you think a friend would want to add to your list.
4. *Highlight what you're particularly proud of.*
   Look at your own list again and highlight or make a star next to the things that you're extra pleased with.
5. *Do a final reflection.*
   Finish by either contemplating on your own or discussing with a friend what it was like to do this exercise. Was there something that was particularly difficult to write down or share, and if so, why do you think that is?

Expose what's difficult

A lot of people find it hard to talk about difficult subjects. Perhaps they don't want to be a burden to others or dampen the mood. When we want to share something difficult, we also have to be more responsive to the *circumstances* compared to when we share something positive. Do we have enough time? Is there a risk that someone could barge in and interrupt? Is the friend open to taking this information in right now?

A common pitfall is to get stuck in rumination. Like a scratched vinyl album that has gotten stuck, we can keep telling the same story time and time again. Another pitfall is that we can talk about difficult matters in a way that our words don't match our emotions or what we're expressing with our bodies and faces. We may laugh or seem unaffected while talking about something really difficult, in an attempt to make ourselves less vulnerable. We hide what feels difficult. We can also make ourselves less vulnerable and thereby less reachable by taking on a victim-role (and thereby ending up in a collapsed state). All these things can make it difficult for others to reach us, and in the worst case, they withdraw.

If you're unsure if what you want to share is too heavy, it can help to also share if you've learned something from this difficulty, or if something good came out of it. Another way is to portion out the hard parts, so that the listener isn't overwhelmed. You can help the person who's listening by saying that you know that this can be hard to hear, and by expressing what you would like for them to do. For example, you could say: 'I'm so grateful that you can bear to listen to this. I don't expect anything more from you than just being here and listening', or 'It would be nice to know if you've ever been through something similar', or 'It would be nice to hear what you think you would have felt if you were in this situation.'

'F***-UP FRIDAYS'

J Artem Henriksson is co-founder of a company that works with organisational development and self-leadership in Stockholm. In his office, they've determined that perfectionism and shame kill creativity, and that honesty and openness pave the way to bigger and better ideas. They have a concept called 'F***-up Fridays', where their employers regularly get to present their worst decisions and actions. He shares how he came up with the idea: 'One day, I got an email from a co-worker that made me jump. In the subject field, she had written: *Welcome to a coffee break with me in the lunchroom on Friday, where I will share with you how I lost the client Lyde (fictitious name)*. At first I was hesitant but then I let her have the meeting. It ended up being one of the most productive coffee breaks we had ever had! It opened the door to new ideas and new routines that have probably saved several deals with clients. The co-worker was completely honest about what had caused her to lose the client and shared five examples that we could all learn from. We all sensed how hard it was for her to share this, and that really made us respect her even more. She was incredibly brave. We all make mistakes, but if we try to hide them, neither we nor others get to learn from them. Today, this person is the manager of her own department, and I think a big reason for that is that she is brave enough to be open and vulnerable – that definitely creates trust.'

Express your appreciation and willingness to connect

'I feel so happy whenever we spend time together!' When we say something like this to a friend, it's as if we are, between the lines, posing the question: *Do you like me as much as I like you?* There is always a risk that our warm feelings aren't answered, and we can therefore feel vulnerable when we, for example, pay someone a compliment. In a similar way, you can feel exposed if, for example, you strike up a conversation with a new colleague or call a friend and ask if they want to get together – what if the wish to connect isn't mutual? At the same time, there are few things that have as much potential to strengthen our bonds as showing our appreciation. Therefore, in the following two exercises, you will practise doing just that.

Reflection exercise: Thank an important person[7]

Purpose: To pave the way to a more profound connection by expressing appreciation
Time required: 5–15 minutes
Method: Writing

Is there anyone who has been extra important to you in your life that you would like to thank? Here are some points for you to reflect on to help you identify the people that have been there for you in different periods of your life, to enable you to express your appreciation of them.

1. *Write down the people who have been there for you.*
   Get out a piece of paper and draw a long line along the middle, from left to right. To the far left, you write 0 years old and to the far right you write your current age. Mark out important milestones to get an overview, and then make a rough draft of the highs and lows throughout your life, like waves. Finally, write down which people have been important to you during these times, for example people who have supported you during a hard time, or been important to you when you've been in a good place.

2. *Express your appreciation of someone verbally.*
   Choose someone you feel grateful for and who you believe could appreciate such a gesture. Now write a thank you letter to that person. Be clear about what they did for you and in which way they contributed to you and your life. Try to be as straightforward and concrete as possible, for example: 'I'm so glad that you believed in me when I was about to drop out of nursing school. I will never forget the night I sat at home spiralling, and you and the crew knocked on my door with a pizza.'

3. *Express your appreciation.*
   Think about *if* and, if so, *how* you would want to convey your gratitude. Perhaps you can send what you wrote down as a text

---

7 Adapted from Mavis Tsai's 'Deepening Relationships' course in the 29k app, www.29k.org.

message, e-mail or letter right away, before you continue reading? If so – do it now! Or maybe you'd rather wait and say it over the phone or face to face when you see them, so that you can get immediate feedback? Another option is to record it and send a video. Either way, decide how and when you are going to deliver your thank you.

Connection game: A final farewell[8]

Purpose: To pave the way to a more profound connection by expressing gratitude
Time required: 5–15 minutes
Method: Verbally, with at least one friend

If you were to never see your friend again – if this were the last time you saw each other – what would you want to say? Try doing this exercise with someone you really care about. That can make it easier to find your way into the game and dare to let all your feelings out. Decide which one of you is going to start being A and who will start as B, and read the instructions before you begin.

1. *Imagine the moment of goodbye.*
   Sit down facing each other. Look at each other while imagining that this is the last time you'll ever see each other. Try to imagine the scenario as vividly as possible. You don't know why you have to say goodbye, there is no apparent reason, but you know that after this moment, you'll never be able to see or even talk to each other again.
2. *Say your final farewell.*
   What do you, A, want to say to B now that it's the last time you'll ever see each other? Say it!
3. *Switch roles.*
   Start over from step 1.
4. *Reflect.*
   Finish the exercise in a way that feels natural to you, perhaps by reflecting together or by a hug.

---

8 Adapted from FAP Workshop 2016 with Mavis Tsai and Robert Kohlenberg.

Let the love of others in[9]

People show their good will and love for us in many different ways. Even common, everyday things – like someone saying hello or asking how we are – are expressions of kindness. When we fully accept such a gift from a friend, by showing our genuine gratitude and joy, we're also giving them something nice back. We affirm that the other person is important to us, and that increases the chance of them wanting to continue sharing their kindness. This brings us closer together. How aware are you of the opportunities you're offered to let in the love of others? And do you cherish these moments? In the following exercise, you will be asked to put on your 'love-glasses'.

Portable tool: On the lookout for love

Purpose: To find opportunities to accept love
Time required: Continuously throughout your everyday life
Method: Mentally

1. *Become a love hawk.*

   Pay extra attention if someone is showing you kindness or appreciation. Remind yourself that this is an opportunity for you to accept this person's affection. It could be something as simple as somebody holding a door open for you, or paying you a compliment. It could also be something bigger, like a friend devoting a whole day to help you move.

2. *Notice how it feels.*

   How does it feel in your body when this happens? What emotions emerge? How much love are you letting in?

3. *Notice how the other person reacts.*

   If you choose to show your appreciation, how does the other person react?

Contemplate with a friend how you usually accept gifts, compliments or other acts of love and kindness from others. Is it easy or hard for you to take in other people's consideration and appreciation? Common

---

9 Adapted from Jonathan Kanter's exercises in the course 'Deepening Relationships' in the 29k app, www.29k.org

obstacles to this can be that you have a history with the person which makes it more difficult, that it feels unfamiliar, or that you're afraid of getting into some kind of gratitude debt. It can also be about not fully trusting that the person genuinely means what they are saying or doing. You may think 'He says that to everyone.' What could prevent you from fully letting the love in? How would you benefit by letting it in more?

In summary

We've all been hurt at some point in our lives. The fear of being hurt again can make us try to hide parts of ourselves, seem perfect or make ourselves so small that we can barely be seen. The strategy of hiding is often brought on by shame. But if we dare to be present and emotionally exposed, chances of creating deeper connections and more trusting relationships increase. If the person listening to us meets us well and takes our hand, we expand our comfort zones so that we slowly, piece by piece, have the courage to show more of our core.

CHAPTER 8
Responsiveness is key

Liam is on the phone with his friend Anna, whose father passed away just a few days ago. Anna is upset and her thoughts and feelings cycle rapidly. Liam feels overwhelmed and has a hard time following, while also trying to find the right thing to say. He's trying to understand what Anna might need to hear, but he's drawing a blank. 'Why have I never been taught how to comfort someone?' he thinks, irritated and concerned. Then he remembers how impressed he was with his young daughter's response a while ago, when her friend took a hard hit from the ball they were playing with. He remembers how natural it seemed. She just stood there, saying 'ooh and aw' while stroking her friend's arm. He realises that the most important thing he can do for Anna now is to not do much at all, but just listen. He gives her his full attention while she continues to talk.

The moment when a friend opens up and is vulnerable is one of the most crucial to determining whether the relationship will deepen, remain at status quo or deteriorate. The A-B-A model describes how moments of deeper connection arise when a person allows themself to be vulnerable and receives a response that is kind and benevolent. (When we hereafter write *'response'*, it is to refer to the other person's reaction and reply in such moments.) In this chapter, we will explore how you can harbour the trust you're given when your friend opens up to you. How can you show your kindness and good favour so that your friend feels safe enough to continue being open and vulnerable?

Hand in hand into the unknown

If you could choose whether your friends were to either withdraw from you or do their best to be there for you when you were going through a crisis, the choice would probably be simple. Nevertheless, it is not entirely uncommon that friends reach out less when we need them the most – for example when we lose a loved one or get a serious illness. Why is that? Perhaps part of the explanation is that we, like Liam in the example above, feel that we have to *perform* when a friend needs our support. We can imagine that we have to say exactly the right thing at the right time, and that we need some kind of expertise to do so.

When a friend shows themself as vulnerable, they take a trembling step into the unknown. To respond well, we need to be brave enough to follow them into these unexplored grounds. As so often in relationships, we then take a risk. We can lose our balance and stumble. We can misunderstand and we can be misunderstood. But we can also meet, and thereby both of us can become less afraid and feel more secure. The best thing we can do is to just be there, in our full, imperfect humanity. We don't need to know (and *can't* know) exactly what will happen, what we should say, or how it will be received, but we can take a minute, make ourselves accessible and listen.

Your response really matters

Jennifer, a friend of one of the authors, has struggled with mental health issues during large parts of her life. She has noticed that it can be difficult for others to meet her when she talks about what she's been through. 'When I had just gotten my diagnosis, I remember that two people reacted very differently. One friend said: "Well, I guess we all have some kind of diagnosis." It felt so casual, almost like she didn't believe me, or that she thought that I was overreacting. I felt disappointed and became silent. After a while I noticed that I was no longer actively seeking her company and we grew apart. Another person, who at that point was just an acquaintance, just said something like: "Damn, that's rough!" and just held me. It was exactly what I needed! I fell into her arms and started to bawl.'

We don't know what the intention of the first friend's response was. Perhaps Jennifer misinterpreted her? Maybe she just meant: 'Hey, we're all a little weird, you're as normal as anyone else.' If Jennifer had told her that the comment didn't land well with her, she would have given the friend a better chance at understanding how hurtful the response was. The damage could have been repaired, and the friendship may have taken a different turn. But the key message here is that the response we get in sensitive moments can make a big difference in determining how the relationship will unfold. In the following exercise, you will get an opportunity to reflect on how other people's responses affect you.

Reflection exercise: Others' response when you've exposed your vulnerability[10]

Purpose: To get an idea of the value of being treated benevolently when you expose yourself as vulnerable

Time required: 3–7 minutes

Method: Writing

1. *Write down some behaviours that cause you to want to open up.*

a) Is there any particular friend or person close to you with whom you feel a special trust and sense of security? What is it in that person's way of treating you that contributes to you feeling this way? Reflect and write down your thoughts.

b) Imagine that you're sharing a sensitive subject with this person. What would they typically do (or refrain from doing) to make you feel comfortable and safe? Write it down, for example: 'Look me in the eye', 'Listen without interrupting', 'Not give me unsolicited advice.'

2. *Write down behaviours that make you want to withdraw and close up.*

a) Is there any particular friend or person close to you with whom you *don't* feel very secure and comfortable? What in this person's way of treating you do you think contributes to you feeling this way? Reflect and write down your thoughts.

---

10 Adapted from Jonathan Kanter's exercises in the course 'Deepening Relationships' in the 29k app, www.29k.org.

b) Imagine that you're sharing a sensitive subject with this person. What would they typically do (or refrain from doing) that would cause you to feel insecure and uncomfortable? Write it down, for example: 'Question me', 'Ignore me', 'Start talking about themselves.'

c) How could this person have met you in a better way? What could they have done differently (or refrained from doing) in order for you to want to continue being open and vulnerable?

Now that you have clarified to yourself which kind of response can promote trust and security for you, you also have an idea of how to meet others in a way that promotes their trust. But remember that it's just a hint – we're all unique individuals, and in different situations we need to be met in different ways.

Treat others as they want to be treated

Have you been taught to treat others as *you* want to be treated? This is often referred to as 'the golden rule'. But applying it doesn't always lead to golden results. Does the fact that your friend wants practical advice when telling you about a work-related problem, mean that he should give you the same when *you* have problems at work? Imagine meeting up with this friend after a long and hard workday. You've just spent eight hours on your feet without a break, waiting on entitled customers. You're mentally exhausted after having been all wound up for the day, and all you need is to unwind, talk through it, and blow off some steam. How would it feel if your friend started blurting out clever suggestions about how to automate the customer reception process?

If you look at your own life, have there been times when your attempts to show appreciation weren't as well received as you had hoped? Perhaps you have treated a friend to a luxury dinner without getting the grateful response that you expected (based on how happy and grateful you yourself would have been for such a gesture). The pastor Gary Chapman attempted to understand this phenomenon. In the 1990s he published his book *The Five Love Languages*, which was a huge hit. He presented the idea that there are different ways of expressing and accepting love. He identified five typical 'love-languages': *Material gifts*, *quality time*, *affirmative words*, *favours* and *physical touch*. Chapman meant that we each have our preferences – we have varying abilities to express and understand each language. Even though the ways of expressing love aren't necessarily limited to these five ways, the message is worth contemplating: We are all different, and when it comes to expressing love, we have a lot to gain by being interested in which types of expressions the receiver actually appreciates.

Since we tend to want to give what we ourselves appreciate (someone who appreciates a deep massage is more inclined to give the same to others), we can be observant of how our friends express love. For example, if a friend sends you a lot of sweet text messages, they probably appreciate getting sweet texts in return. A friend who makes sure to call you on your birthday probably appreciates a call on their own birthday. But we all like and need different things at different times, and love languages are not like blood types which never change. Sometimes you may be more than happy to accept your friend's good advice, while other times, advice is the last thing you need. Sometimes your friend wants help to improve their mood, while other times, they just want to share their sadness.

In Chapter 6, *Entering your friend's world*, we wrote about how we can improve our skills in understanding our friends. Asking open-ended questions, listening profoundly, and being curious about how *your friend* wants to be treated. Instead of *assuming* that you know, you can *wonder* – what might your friend need right now?

Ask what your friend needs

A common mistake is that we give tips and advice when our friend just wants to be heard and accepted. 'Don't be sad', 'That wasn't so bad, was it?', or 'Hey, think of it like this instead . . . ' Sometimes, comments like that can unintentionally signal 'You mustn't feel what you're feeling', or even 'You're incapable of figuring this out on your own.' Sometimes we're asked for our input, and in those cases it's of course OK, but quite often our opinion is not what's wanted or needed. If we instead listen and are interested in our friend's experience, the chances are greater that we convey: 'I accept you the way you are.' In turn, this can pave the way for your friend to find new perspectives and solutions on their own.

Since many of us have an exaggerated focus on solving problems, it can be wise to at least wait a little before trying to do so. If you begin with assuming that what your friend wants is emotional support, you can always switch over to problem-solving later, if it turns out that that's what your friend wants. But you can also simply ask: 'Do you want my opinion about all of this or do you just want me to listen?' or 'Is it OK that I'm asking so many questions about this?', or 'I really want to hear more about this, but I'm feeling afraid of saying the wrong things. Can I just listen?'

Talk with your body

Although we usually want what's best for our friends, we're not always great at communicating that. Imagine that someone is sharing something sensitive with you, and while they're talking, your eyes start to wander, you check your phone and fiddle with your pen. This person will most likely perceive that you're restless or uninterested. A behaviour like this will make most people want to quickly change the subject or stop talking. If you instead look them in the eye and reflect their feelings with your facial expressions, you send a completely different message – that you're listening and that you care.

Turning towards and looking at the person you're talking to also helps you maintain your focus. If you also allow yourself to let down your guard and show your natural emotional expressions, it will be easier for your friend to interpret and understand your intentions. The probability is high that your friend will feel more *secure* with you if you're able to be open with what *you* feel. Below is an exercise that quickly gives you a sense of this dynamic.

Connection game: Still eyebrows[11]

Purpose: To explore how your facial expressions affect your connection to others
Time required: 2 minutes
Method: Verbally with at least one friend

1. *Say hello to each other.*
   Greet each other as if you hadn't seen each other in years and are really happy to be reunited!
2. *Say hello to each other with still eyebrows.*
   Re-enact the same situation again, but this time keep your eyebrows completely still when you greet each other. Really make sure that they don't move!
3. *Talk to each other about how you experienced the difference.*
   How was it to greet each other when you could and could not 'use' your eyebrows?

Say that you can relate

An efficient and rather common way of making a friend feel insecure when they're telling you something sensitive, is to hijack the conversation and start talking about something completely different. How would it have been for Anna if Liam, in the introductory example, had cut her off to talk about how as a teenager he lost a distant relative and wasn't very affected by it? Most likely, Anna would have felt neither seen nor understood. But sharing your own experiences in an *empathetic* manner can be a way of showing that you understand, and that you can relate to what your friend is talking about.

Imagine that you're revealing to a friend how frustrating you think it is when you don't understand your new colleagues' inside jokes. You explain that this pretty much happens on a daily basis, and that you feel at a loss for words and excluded. If your friend had had similar experiences, would you want to hear about them? How would it feel

---

11 This exercise comes from *radically open dialectical behavior therapy* (RO-DBT).

if they had said: 'You know what, I actually had the exact same experience at my last job. It was really hard!'? When you relate to what you've heard and share a similar experience of your own, it can be like indirectly saying: 'You're not alone' and 'We have something in common.' The crucial aspect is that you share your own experience out of consideration for the other person, and not as a way of taking over and making the conversation about you.

Another way to contribute to a deeper connection is by sharing something that you're experiencing in the moment, while you're with the other person. If you notice yourself feeling genuinely touched by what your friend is telling you – say it! Maybe you notice that you're feeling grateful that they're sharing something so sensitive with you – say that too! If you have the courage to put words to the direct emotional impact your friend has on you, you make yourself more accessible, while also sending a clear signal that your friend is important to you.

Both supportive and sincere

Is it necessary to agree with each other in order to have a close connection? Say your friend reacts strongly to something you consider to be trivial. Perhaps your friend gained five pounds and sees this as a big failure. You get a strong impulse to explain that it's really not that big of a deal: 'So what, you have a healthy and beautiful body, what's the point of obsessing over a few pounds?' You really don't find it *reasonable* that your friend is focusing so much on their body weight. Should you disregard your own conviction in order to validate your friend? What should you prioritise, your integrity or the bond with your friend? Do these even need to be conflicting matters?

From the other's point of view

Imagine for a moment that you had come into this world with the exact same set of genes as your friend, and that you had walked in their shoes your whole life. Wouldn't you then have reacted in about (or exactly) the same way if you had gained weight? If you can see and convey that it's *understandable* that your friend thinks and feels as they do, you don't necessarily have to compromise your own beliefs and take on your friend's idea of reality in order to respond well. Maybe it's enough to look at the situation from your friend's point of reference. You could for example say: 'Ah, I think we have different views about our bodies. Could you please tell me more about why you think that this is so important to you?'

Supporting without agreeing

In our everyday lives, we often habitually merge our inner experiences (emotions) with descriptions and interpretations of our outside world (our surrounding environment). We talk about *feeling* offended, we *feel* that we're not listened to, and so on. In the previously mentioned giraffe language, non-violent communication (NVC), these are referred to as *emotional thoughts*. If you, for example, say that you 'feel distrusted' by someone, you're not actually saying what emotion you're experiencing – just that you *perceive* that the other person doesn't believe you. Whether or not the other person actually distrusts you is for them to say, but only you know how you're actually *feeling*. In this particular scenario, it could, for example, be fear or anger.

Distinguishing between emotions and emotional thoughts is essential in NVC. It can take some practice, but the more you practise, the more skilled you become in responding to others without having to either compromise your own beliefs or agree with theirs. Here, the ability to *listen deeply* comes in handy. Imagine that your friend says that he's sick of your mutual friend Karen being so self-absorbed. You, on the other hand, rather think that Karen is very responsive and empathetic, and therefore you don't want to corroborate your friend's view of her. However, you still want to convey that you're taking in what your friend is saying and that you care about him. One way of doing that is to listen deeply and show an interest in the emotions behind the words, and perhaps saying something like 'I'm hearing that it's hard for you to not feel seen – is that correct?' When your friend feels listened to, it's easier for him to take in your honesty: 'I want to support you and help you find a solution, but from my perspective, I can't relate to your description of Karen. I feel she is very open and responsive.' Otherwise, empathy without honesty can easily be perceived as agreeing.

Connection game: See, ask and give

Purpose: a) To practise listening deeply and responding well
b) To become aware of what kind of response you want from each other and to practise asking for it
Time required: 15–30 minutes
Method: Verbally, with a friend

Read the full instructions before you start and decide which one of you will start being person A and who will be person B. Have a timer at hand.

1. *A shares something sensitive.*

   For example, person A can share something that they're struggling with, something they're longing for, or something they rarely talk to others about.

2. *B listens deeply.*

   By listening deeply to both *what* is being said and *how* it is said, person B tries to comprehend A's feelings and needs. They can hum and nod, but not say anything while A is talking.

3. *Set your timer to one minute.*

   When person A is finished, they say 'done', and person B just says, 'thank you'. Then you set the timer to one minute, during which you are both completely silent. Person A contemplates what kind of response they would like from B.

4. *B asks what A wants or needs.*

   After the minute of silence is over, B asks what A would like to hear or what kind of response they would appreciate. A answers the question, for example: 'Get advice', 'Hear that I'm not weird for feeling the way I do', 'Hear if you can relate to what I've just said.'

5. *B gives the response that A asked for.*

   Person B tries to respond to A's wishes as much as possible, without crossing their own boundaries of what feels right.

6. *B asks again.*

   B checks if A wants or needs to hear anything else and, if so, keeps responding.

7. *Reflect.*

   Take a few minutes to share your experiences with each other. How was it for person A to share, be listened to and ask for a particular response? How was it for B to listen and respond?

8. *Switch roles and start over.*

More than words

Have you ever been comforted without words? Or have you experienced a strong and nice connection with someone when you were both silent? Most people sense that the most important thing isn't about *saying* the right things but about being mentally and emotionally present, yet this is something that we seem to forget. Liam, in the introductory example, forgot this, until he remembered how his daughter had comforted her friend. Our hope is that the following exercise will serve as a reminder of how much can be said without words.

Connection game: See and be seen[12]

Purpose: To explore how it feels to see and be seen without words
Time required: 3–5 minutes
Method: Wordless, with a friend

Read the instructions and decide who will start as person A and who will start as person B. Have a timer at hand.

1. *A looks at B for one minute.*

   Set a timer to one minute and sit across from each other. Person A, you should give B your full attention. Look into B's eyes and

---

12 This exercise is adapted from The Connection Institute's Relational Leadership Program.

show that you are truly interested in seeing and taking in all of B. You can say silently to yourself: 'I see you _____ ' (fill the blank with person B's name). Person B has one single task here: Allowing yourself to be seen. Notice how it feels and how much of yourself you are willing to expose.

2. *Switch roles for one minute.*

3. *See and be seen for one minute.*

   In the end, you can try to both see each other and allow yourselves to be seen simultaneously; that is, focus part of your attention on yourself and part of your attention on the other person.

4. *Discuss your experiences.*

   What did you notice? How was it to be seen? How was it to see the other person? How did you experience the difference?

Perhaps this exercise will make you more aware of how much you typically focus on yourself and how much you tend to focus on others. Some of us may find it hard or unfamiliar to allow ourselves to be seen. If that applies to you, we encourage you to let your focus shift smoothly back and forth between yourself and your friend. A flexible focus almost always has a clarifying effect – we become more aware of both our own and our friends' feelings and needs.

Be on the lookout for vulnerability

It's usually easy to recognise when someone takes a *big*, courageous step or is *very* vulnerable, but the *small* moments of vulnerability are often overlooked. It can be something as simple as your friend telling you about a failed cooking project or somebody apologising for being late to an important meeting. We may not even notice when *we ourselves* are a little brave in this way. Most of us are good at more or less consciously disregarding both our own and others' vulnerability. By being on the lookout and acknowledging situations where someone is even a little vulnerable, you can catch unexpected opportunities for responding well, and in that way deepen your connection with others.

Portable tool: On the lookout for vulnerability[13]

Purpose: Increasing your awareness of when others take brave steps
Time required: Continuously throughout your everyday life
Method: Mentally

1. *Be on the lookout for vulnerability.*

   Pay extra attention when others expose themselves in vulnerability, and remind yourself that these moments are important. It could be something small, like someone making eye contact, saying that they like something about you, or wanting to buy you lunch. It could also be something bigger, like someone asking for forgiveness, sharing a difficult matter or asking you for help.
2. *Notice how it feels.*

   How does your body feel? What emotions are awakened?
3. *Notice how you respond.*

   How do you respond to the other person in that moment?
4. *Notice how the other person reacts to your response.*

   How does the other person seem to be affected by your response?

Is there anything that you would like to do differently? We encourage you to discuss this theme with a friend. What does your friend do in these situations and what do they think about this? Do they usually notice when others are vulnerable? What do they find important when it comes to responding to someone who is vulnerable?

---

13 This exercise is inspired by Jonathan Kanter's exercises in the course 'Deepening Relationships' in the 29k app, www.29k.org.

In summary

Out of all the things that happen in a relationship, there is one moment that is particularly essential to whether or not the relationship will deepen: when one person opens up and is vulnerable to the other. If the person who has opened up feels that they are met with kindness and empathy, chances are that their trust will increase and that they will dare to expose even more of themselves. Sometimes we make the mistake of thinking that a good response means that we have to say something smart or wise. In fact, it's enough to just pause, make eye contact and be present with our friend in the moment.

CHAPTER 9
Transforming conflicts

Around five o'clock on a Friday evening, Robert contacts his long-time best friend Linda and asks if she wants to get together. Linda is worn out, and thinks that a calm evening at home with Robert sounds perfect. Robert, on the other hand, has been home with a head cold for a few days and has finally regained his strength. He's up for some fun and is happy when Linda invites him over to her place. He texts back: 'Great! I'll be over soon!' Robert figures that he has time to stop by the record shop before heading over to Linda's place. There, he bumps into William, another old friend. They revisit their favourite music together, and time flies by. William shares that he is recently separated and feeling pretty lonely, so Robert invites him to tag along to Linda's. When Robert and William knock on her door, it's almost seven o'clock. She has prepared a soup that is now cold, and her small kitchen table is nicely set for two. 'I brought an extra guest who needs some cheering up!' Robert jokes, and introduces William. Linda is clearly irritated and thinks to herself: 'Why did it take him two hours to get here when he said he'd be over "soon", and why bring a stranger without checking first?'

Conflicts seem to be inevitable in relationships. As most of us have experienced, friendships are no exception. We three authors are Swedish and it's sometimes said that we Swedes avoid conflict like the plague, and in many contexts, that may be wise. However, if we always flee when friction arises, we might miss opportunities to get to know each other on a deeper level.

The word 'conflict' comes from the Latin word *conflictus*, meaning to clash, impact, or collide. In every collision, energy is released. If you've ever seen a toddler throw a tantrum, you may have been surprised by the incredible force an unfulfilled will can generate in such a small body. What would you think and feel if you saw an adult act in the same way? If we don't convert our energy into something more useful than flipping out, we risk ruining relationships. But suffocating the energy – wouldn't that be a lost opportunity? As you may remember from your early physics classes in school, no energy can disappear from our universe – it can only be converted. So instead of asking ourselves how we can *solve* conflicts, maybe we can explore how we can *use* the energy to deepen our connection.

In this chapter, we will discuss some strategies and approaches that can help us deepen our relationships when conflicts arise – how we can turn sand into pearls. But first, we will look into what usually causes conflict in friendships.

Common causes of conflict

In Chapter 2, *A formula for friendship*, we summarised the research about what's important in order to maintain close friendships: *time together, positivity, similarity, reciprocity, loyalty* and *openness*. Conversely, friendships can be weakened, or even threatened, if the relationship is lacking in one or several of these aspects. In the research of psychologist Mary Parlee, she found two main reasons for friendships weakening or ceasing: *betrayal* and *conflicting values*. When we authors asked people in our networks about what had caused friction in their friendships, we were given the following answers:

Different interests, values and expectations
> When we grew apart and developed different interests.
> When we had completely opposing opinions about something important.
> When we had different expectations about how often we should talk or get together.

Lack of reciprocity

When the other person didn't listen to me, and instead just talked about themself.

When the other person only contacted me when they needed something from me.

When the other person wasn't open and vulnerable (as I was) and only showed their good sides.

When the other person stopped taking my calls after starting a romantic relationship with a new partner.

Lack of loyalty

When the other person wasn't happy for me, but instead reacted with jealousy when I succeeded in some way.

When the other person wasn't there for me when I needed help or support.

When the other person spoke badly of me or of my family and close friends.

Four good ways of dealing with friction

Do you recognise any of these causes of friction in your own relationships, current or past? What are ways to avoid or to deal with them? We will now explore four key strategies for managing conflict in friendships. First, we will take a look at how conflicts and misunderstandings can be *avoided*. Next, we look at ways to address irritations and increase the chances of the relationship being strengthened once conflicts arise. We then discuss when it is better to give up on your attempts to change these issues, either by accepting them and *leaving them*, or, as a last resort, by *breaking up* and ending the friendship.

Avoid unnecessary conflict

One of the main causes of misunderstandings and conflicts is a collision between our unspoken expectations. The following section is about how we, by *clarifying* our expectations, can reduce the risk of this type of conflict even arising in the first place.

Unspoken expectations can lead to misunderstandings

We all have a vast number of unspoken expectations. For instance, we assume that the floor will carry our weight when we get out of bed in the morning, and that the water we use to make our morning coffee isn't going to poison us. Pretty much everything we do is based on our expectations, and social situations are no exception. There are rules that are stated (you bike on the correct side of the road, you don't steal from others, and so on), but many (most?) are *unspoken*. We've simply had to learn from experience what kinds of behaviours work in different contexts, and thereby it usually goes pretty smoothly. For example, you don't cancel a badminton game with a friend twenty minutes before your scheduled time, just because you felt like going to the cinema with another friend. Right?

In the introductory example of this chapter, Linda took for granted that the plan for the evening was to just chill and relax, while Robert was set on some party action. For Robert, the word *soon* meant 'later tonight', whereas Linda thought it meant the 20 minutes that it would take Robert to walk to her place. Furthermore, Linda took for granted that it was just going to be Robert and herself, whereas Robert found it completely natural to invite William to come along. What do you think would have happened if Robert and Linda had discussed in advance what their expectations of the evening were?

Clarify your expectations before getting together

Since unspoken expectations often lead to misunderstandings, an efficient way of becoming more compatible and united is to be direct about your expectations beforehand. For instance, before getting together, we can touch base to make sure that we agree about who is going to be there, what we want to do, and maybe even why we want to do it. The following five questions can serve as a guide to clarify the boundaries to pretty much every kind of social interaction: *Why? What? Who? When? Where?*

Here is an illustration of how Robert's and Linda's colliding expectations could have been clarified using these questions:

Why? What is the purpose of getting together?
Robert *wanted excitement and fun, while Linda was looking forward to a quiet and calm evening together.*
What? What are we going to do?
Robert *wanted to pre-party a little and then go out, while Linda had a cosy evening at home in mind, with dinner and maybe a movie.*
Who? Who is going to participate?
Robert *thought 'the more, the merrier', while Linda expected it to be just the two of them.*
When? When and for how long are we getting together?
Robert *thought they'd get together at some point during the evening to hang out until around midnight, while Linda thought that Robert would be coming over right away, and then hang out until around 10 pm.*
Where? Where are we getting together?
Robert *wanted to meet up at Linda's place and then head out to town, while Linda was thinking of a more calm environment – first at home and then maybe a walk in the nearby park.*

The question of *why* is particularly relevant. It's often neglected, either because we don't really know the answer or because we think it's so obvious that it doesn't need to be specified – 'you get together to have a good time'. But what does 'a good time' mean? Apparently, it means different things to different people. And different things to the same person at different times. Since the *purpose* of getting together often determines the kind of interaction, answering the question of *why* can also help us answer the other questions (about *what* we are going to do, *when*, *where*, and with *whom* we are going to do it).

Clarify your expectations of the relationship

'Why don't you ever call me? Why am I always the one taking the initiative to get together?' Just as our expectations of a get-together can vary, so can our expectations of the relationship as a whole. In dating contexts, we are often keen on quickly trying to figure out 'where we stand', if the other person is looking for something serious or just a fling, and so on. We simply try to clarify each other's expectations and hopes. Friendships, on the other hand, often just continue without anyone ever discussing such matters. One person may expect to get together regularly, whereas the other person thinks that getting together a few times a year is enough. It never needs to be expressed and clarified and also doesn't need to be an issue. Unspoken expectations of friendships don't necessarily lead to conflict. But are there any of your relationships that could benefit from the two of you being a little more clear and straightforward with each other?

Things that can be worth discussing are, for example: How often the two of you expect to get together, how you want to deal with money (do you take turns treating each other or do you split equally each time?), if it's OK to date each other's ex-partners, how important it is to be on time, or if there are any special circumstances (for example diets, disabilities or specific needs) that need to be taken into consideration?

Behind incompatible wills there are compatible needs

Sometimes, *clarifying* unspoken expectations isn't enough to prevent conflict – some wishes just aren't compatible. For instance, Robert's will to party wasn't compatible with Linda's will to relax. How do we deal with conflicting wills? By letting the strongest and most stubborn person have their way? By compromising?

The giraffe language (non-violent communication, NVC) mentioned earlier is a conflict management method that strives to fulfil *everyone's* needs. We will now present one of the key aspects of this method: distinguishing between *needs* and *strategies*. According to NVC, needs are distinguished by not being tied to a certain person, place, act or time. What characterises *needs* is also that they can be met by applying a number of different strategies. The point of distinguishing clearly between the two is to make it easier to see how several strategies can be applied to meet the same need. For example, if you're *in need* of company, you could call your family, but you could also knock on your neighbour's door, or visit a friend.

In this chapter's introductory example, it's clear that Linda and Robert want to do different things. But if you were to try to identify their *needs*, what would you guess? Let's say that Linda's needs are *rest* and *company*, and Robert's needs are *company, spontaneity* and *fun*. How would they be able to meet all of their needs without compromise or coercion? There are many different ways. For starters, they both have a need for company. By following Linda's original plan to get together at her place, that need would have been met for both of them. The calm environment in her home would also have allowed Linda the rest that she needed. When it comes to Robert, he could have fulfilled his need for fun and partying *after* his dinner with Linda. Surely, there are numerous different ways that they could have planned their evening so that they both got what they needed, including the option of spending the evening apart.

The example above illustrates the principle that everyone's needs can be fulfilled, if we figure out the underlying needs, and are creative about looking for compatible strategies, without blindly focusing on one specific solution. Even if we don't succeed in finding compatible strategies, the *ambition* to do so can help avoid unnecessary conflict.

Address the issue causing friction

No matter how good we are, or get, at avoiding conflicts, it's hard to see how we could ever fully avoid them. So, when we sense some irritation, or once conflict arises, what do we do? Do we silently clench our fists and make the other person out to be 'the bad guy' in our head? ('She ought to understand that she can't do stuff like that' or 'Doesn't he see that I need some space, too?') Or do we tone the whole thing down? Or do we withdraw?

What if we were to see it as a gift to our relationship to address these issues and talk about them? If we move towards the other person and the difficult matter instead of drawing back? Conflicts *are* difficult. They activate our inner fears and quite often bring out the worst in us. But if we manage to remain humble instead of collapsing in shame or becoming arrogant, we see each other in a different, clearer light. Ideally, through the conflict, we take our friendship to a new level. So how do we succeed in doing that? In order to keep in touch with each other we need to keep in touch with ourselves. Therefore, the challenge lies in allowing ourselves to fully feel what we feel, including being open to discomfort and unpleasantness. The following exercise will give you and a friend the opportunity to experiment with this in a playful way.

Connection game: Get comfortable being uncomfortable[14]

Purpose: To practise maintaining your connection even when you experience discomfort
Time required: 10–20 minutes
Method: You, a friend and a timer

Start by reading the instructions and agreeing on a time frame – this determines how intense the exercise will be. A suitable and pretty challenging time limit is 15 minutes.

1. *Set a timer.*
2. *Take your positions.*
   Stand face to face, about a yard apart. Bend your knees, as if you were to sit down on a chair but stopped half way (if you can't hold this position throughout the entire exercise, you may of course adjust your positions). The point is to be really uncomfortable and even in pain.
3. *Maintain full connection and presence with the other person and with yourself.*
   Look each other in the eyes. See if you can welcome, instead of fighting, all the emotions and physical sensations that emerge, while maintaining eye contact the whole time.
4. *When the time is up, you finish and stand up.*
5. *Reflect together.*

Take a moment to talk to each other about what you experienced. Were you able to remain open and present despite the burning pain in your legs? Or did the pain make it more difficult? If you noticed that you

---

14 This exercise comes from the course 'Authentic Relating Training International – level 2', held by ART International.

were able to maintain your connection – what could that imply about your opportunities to remain connected during a conflict situation?

When *you* address the cause of the friction

When you want to talk about something that's bothering you, there are a few steps that you can take to reduce the risk of it resulting in a conflict. The first is to ask yourself: 'Is it important to bring this up?' or 'What is my purpose in saying this?' If you come to the conclusion that it wasn't that important, or that you mostly wanted to say it to snap at your friend in revenge, there are probably better ways of dealing with your feelings. But if it's important for you both to continue your friendship, you can remind yourself of this shortly before or while you're bringing it up. This can help you maintain your focus on nurturing the relationship (rather than, for example, 'being right'). Another step is to check with your friend if they're accessible and if the timing is right. Do they have the time and energy needed to have this conversation? Yet another step is to reduce the risk of insecurity and misunderstandings by being as open as you can, both with *why* you're bringing this up, and with *how it feels* for you to do so. If you're clear about your intentions and emotions, your friend is more likely to also feel secure, which creates better conditions for mutual understanding.

Behind these difficult emotions, there often lie needs that haven't been met. In the passage below, we will provide a more detailed account of how you can express these feelings in a way that promotes connection instead of complicating it.

Express what you want and need

Expressing our needs or setting boundaries in a good way can be an art form. Three common mistakes are that we 1) only focus on the other person, 2) claim that the other person *is* a certain way, and 3) bring up old wrongdoings and totally irrelevant things that bother us. It could sound something like this: 'You're so selfish, you're never on time, and whenever we do something together, I'm always the one who has to deal with all the preparations.' Besides creating unnecessary irritation in the person being labelled as 'selfish', it makes it hard to react constructively since it's the *person* rather than the *behaviour* that is being criticised. One key that a lot of readers have probably heard is to try to use *I-statements* when talking about a difficult topic. When we use I-statements, we own our accusations. We focus on ourselves and what we feel, and we express how we're affected by the other's behaviour rather than by their personality. It could sound something like this: 'I get sad and angry when you don't arrive on time.'

If we furthermore express *what we would like* from the other person and connect that to a *need*, it becomes much easier for them to understand what we need, and how they can accommodate that need. For example, we could say: 'I feel sad and angry when you don't arrive on time, since I need to use my time efficiently. From now on, I would really appreciate it if you could contact me and let me know if you're going to be late.' The request should be as straightforward and 'doable' as possible. Compare 'I would like you to acknowledge me more' to 'I would appreciate it if you asked more questions about me.' Which of the wishes would be easiest for you to accommodate?

Another aspect is that it feels better to give a person what they want if they *ask* for it rather than if they *demand* it. The difference between an inquiry and a demand is whether or not we can accept *no* as an answer. If we punish someone (for example by snapping back at them, accusing them or becoming passive aggressive), we probably made a demand. Sooner or later, demands give a bitter aftertaste, and create distance between us.

The textbook example of an empathetic and clearly expressed inquiry sounds something like this: 'When you do X, I feel Y, because I need Z. Therefore, I would like Q.' Naturally, we rarely express ourselves exactly like that, but with a little practice, we can remember the most important part: Taking responsibility for our experience and our feelings, and expressing our wishes in a concrete way without punishing the other person if they don't accommodate them. The following exercise will help you think about how you could express your needs in such a way.

Reflection exercise: Asking without demanding[15]

Purpose: To practise expressing your needs and desires without demanding anything or accusing the other person

Time required: 5–10 minutes

Method: Writing

If you want, this exercise can be seen as a preparation for expressing your wants and needs at a later time.

1. *Choose an important relationship that has some aspect that bothers you.*
   Think about if you have a relationship where something doesn't feel quite right.
2. *Write down what you appreciate about that person and your relationship.*
   What do you like about this person? What do they contribute to your life?
3. *Get in touch with your feelings.*
   Think about a particularly difficult situation, or of the routine you have with this person that doesn't feel quite right. Try to make space for the emotions that arise. Allow yourself to feel them in your entire body. Then write down the most prominent emotions.
4. *Write down your underlying needs.*
   Think about which underlying need(s) trigger(s) these emotions. For example, if you feel sad or frustrated that your friend doesn't ask about what's going on in your life, the underlying need could be: 'Feeling seen and appreciated.'
5. *Write down a request that is tied to these needs.*
   a) Express your request as clearly and concretely as possible, by thinking about what you would like the other person to do. For example: 'I would like you to ask me more frequently how my day was, and give me time to answer' (rather than 'I wish you'd stop being so self-absorbed').

---

15 Adapted from Jonathan Kanter's exercise 'Make Your Needs Known' in the course Deepening Relationships in the 29k app, www.29k.org.

b) Now add *why* this is important to you, by expressing which *needs* would be accommodated if your request were to be fulfilled. For example: ' . . . because I have a need to feel seen and appreciated.' This makes it easier for the other person to understand why you're asking for it.

c) Finally, add a question about whether the person wants and is able to accommodate your request. For example: 'How does that sound? Would it be possible? How does it feel for you when I ask for this?'

6. *Listen to your own words.*

Now read your request out loud to yourself and notice how it feels to hear it.

7. *Change your perspective.*

Read what you've written again. This time, think about what the recipient might think or feel upon hearing your request. Could they feel hurt, attacked or accused?

8. *Express yourself in a balanced way.*

If you saw things differently when you changed your perspective, you can rephrase.

Would you now be willing to express your request to this friend? If so, choose an appropriate time. Whether or not you use the specific phrasing that you wrote down, try to connect your want to a need. As we wrote earlier, this can make it easier for the person to understand what lies behind your request, which in turn increases the chance of them feeling empathetic and wanting to accommodate it. After having stated your request, ask your friend how it felt to hear, and ask if anything was unclear, or if there are any unresolved feelings still lingering.

Dealing with a no

Regardless of how well you express your desires, you will occasionally get a no. Imagine if Linda (in this chapter's introductory example) had asked Robert to state exactly what time he was going to be there. If Robert had replied that he didn't want to do that, it would most likely be unnatural for Linda to just accept his refusal. At the same time, she can't force Robert. So how could she have proceeded?

Instead of letting the negative response kill all further attempts at meeting your desire, you can ask the other person why they don't want to (or cannot) accommodate your request. Linda could wonder 'Why don't you want to decide an exact time to get together?' and show an interest in Robert's need which caused him to refuse her request. Without making any demands, she could try to figure out what, if anything, could make it possible for Robert to agree to a specific time.

When *your friend* addresses the cause of the friction

How can you maintain your humility and dignity when your friend brings up something that's bothering them? By seeing all criticism as potentially valuable information, it becomes a gift. You may have had a blind spot that your friend can help you see? It may be easier said than done, but if you succeed in having this approach, it can contribute to stronger relationships as well as to your own personal development. You can basically ask yourself: 'What is it that my friend is trying to say?', 'What is important here?', and 'Why are they bringing this up?'

Below are two tools that can be applied when receiving potentially difficult feedback. The first one, *conversational aikido*, can be used when you feel attacked, criticised or accused. The second one, *the brave question*, is for you to use when you yourself are asking for feedback.

Portable tool: Conversational aikido[16]

Purpose: To maximise the connection when you feel that you're being attacked
Time required: 5–60 minutes
Method: In conversation with a friend

Aikido is a martial art where you use the opponent's energy. When you're attacked, you redirect the force directed at yourself to your own advantage. Hence, we use the metaphor of aikido to describe the art of

---

16 This exercise is inspired by The Aikido Model that was introduced in the book *Conflict = Energy: The Transformative Practice of Authentic Relating*, by Jason Digges.

receiving tough feedback. If you defend yourself or counterattack, you add to the anger. If you instead allow the other person to fully express their frustration, it usually decreases, slowly but surely. When the other person feels that they have been seen and heard, they are better equipped to take in your thoughts and feelings.

In this exercise, we assume that you want to maintain a close relationship and that you don't want to hurt the other person.

1. *Be present.*
   Stop what you're doing and prepare yourself to listen. Make eye contact and show that you are accessible and receptive.
2. *Listen deeply.*
   Listen attentively to what the other person is saying – even if you feel that their criticism is unjustified. If necessary, ask them questions to clarify their feelings and needs. Remind yourself that your intention is to remain connected and nurture the relationship, not to be right or to maintain your self-image as a perfect person.
3. *Repeat and summarise.*
   Using your own words, repeat what you've heard back to the other person, to make sure that you've understood correctly (even if you may not agree). For example, you could say: 'So, what I'm hearing is . . . '
4. *Ask if there's more.*
   Ask if there's anything else that the other person would like to add. If so, repeat the steps above.
5. *Take responsibility.*
   Ask yourself if the other person could be right and have a point in what they're saying (even if it's just something small). If so, try to admit that and take responsibility for it by accepting the criticism. Show that you see your part in all this, and if it feels reasonable – apologise.
6. *Tell them how you feel.*
   Check with the other person if it's OK that you now share your view of the criticism and how it feels to receive it. If the timing is right, try to do so without placing blame or becoming defensive.

Portable tool: The brave question

Purpose: To become aware of what the other person perceives as an obstacle to a closer connection with you
Time required: 2–20 minutes
Method: In conversation with a friend

A powerful tool for finding out what's standing in the way of a deeper connection is to simply ask the question straight out. When we authors have done this with our friends, partners and family members, we've often received valuable information. For instance, we have been inspired to be more clear in expressing our gratitude towards a partner, to not question a friend's illness, and to not be so impatient when on the phone with a parent.

The point isn't necessarily that you have to change or solve whatever it is that's standing in the way. Sometimes, just raising the question can loosen the locks. Inviting your friend to have a conversation about this on the relational level (as described in Chapter 7, *Vulnerable and reachable*) shows that you take the relationship seriously. Be sure to only ask the question if (or when) you feel genuinely interested in hearing your friend's answer.

1. *Pick the right time.*
   Ensure that the context is right so that you both have enough time and energy to clarify the implication of the answer and to process possible emotional consequences.
2. *Ask the question to your friend.*
   Ask your friend something along the lines of: 'What do you think stands in the way of our relationship?' A more charged version of the question is: 'What in my behaviour do you think is the biggest obstacle for our connection?'
3. *Listen and ask clarifying, supplementary questions.*
   Try to listen with curiosity and without immediately getting defensive. Ask follow-up questions if something is unclear to you.

Asking brave questions like this will most likely not only give you ideas about how you can deepen your relationship, but also give you new insights about yourself.

Clarify misunderstandings

Misunderstandings can often be avoided by clarifying unspoken expectations. However, we sometimes still end up in situations where we don't feel that we understand each other. In cases like this, the following exercise may be very helpful. It's been named after Alan Turing, who in the 1950s created a test to determine whether or not a computer could be considered to be intelligent. Computers passed the Turing test if they could answer people's arbitrary questions in such a human-like way that the person posing the question wasn't able to distinguish if the answer (in written form) came from a computer or a human. In a similar way, it is the listener's task in this exercise to repeat the main idea of what the other person has said in such a fair and convincing way that an outsider wouldn't be able to distinguish if they are speaking from their own or their friend's perspective. There are no guarantees that consensus will be reached, but that isn't the point. However, it *does* create good conditions for clearing up misunderstandings and fully understanding each other's perspective.

Portable tool: Turing turns

Purpose: To maximise the chances of mutual understanding
Time required: 15–90 minutes
Method: Verbally with a friend

In this exercise, you and your friend take turns speaking without being interrupted. When one person has finished, the other person (who has listened) repeats the essence of what they've heard. This exercise can be used in a specific conflict ('I don't understand why you didn't come to my birthday party'). It can also be used to clear the air and bring up issues that have caused a more long-term disharmony that isn't related to any specific incident.

1. *Touch base about why you're doing this.*

   Remind yourselves about the purpose of the exercise: To understand each other as well as possible (without necessarily agreeing).

2. *Make sure that you agree on what it is that you want to sort out.*

   For example: 'Why person A didn't reach out to person B more often when he/she was going through X', 'How person A felt when person B said X', 'Why it's important to person A that person B doesn't do X.'

3. *Decide who is going to start talking (person A) and who will start listening (person B).*

   It usually feels most natural to let the person who felt the most affected by the conflict start talking.

4. *Agree on a time frame.*

   a) How much time are you going to spend on this exercise? Anything between 15 minutes and an hour and a half can be appropriate. The quality of the meeting – how mentally and emotionally present you can be – is more important than the actual amount of time you spend.

   b) Decide how long each of you will get to speak without interruption, and who will set the timer. We suggest that you start with about 5 minutes, but allow each other to finish if the timer rings in the middle of a sentence.

5. *A speaks without interruption and B listens deeply.*

   Person A begins to share their perspective. They should try to focus as much as possible on the heart of the matter. If A notices that there is something they're thinking about but avoiding mentioning, it's probably something worth bringing up. Person B doesn't say anything while A is talking, but focuses on listening to the essence of what is being said. What is important to A? Which needs and emotions are being communicated?

6. *B repeats the essence.*

   When A is done with their first round, B gets a few minutes to repeat what they've perceived. The goal is to try to really do justice to A's narrative, without including B's own opinions and perspectives.

7. *A corrects B.*

If A thinks that B has left out something important, they can ask for clarification. For example: 'Can you repeat how I felt when you didn't show up at my party?'

8. *Switch roles and repeat numbers 5–7.*

When A feels that B has repeated the essence of their narrative, you switch roles and repeat the points above. Take turns listening and speaking a few rounds, until you both feel that you've been understood and that you've understood the other person.

Accepting the sources of irritation

It's natural to sometimes get annoyed with our friends. It could be small things in the person's behaviour that irritate us, but that we for different reasons don't want to bring up. Sometimes it's because we think it's really no big deal, and other times it's because we don't have the energy needed to address the issue. A third reason is that we simply don't believe that the person will want to, or be able to, change what it is that's bothering us. Nevertheless, our inner frustration with our friend's behaviour can linger like a veil between us. If we are too preoccupied with our own thoughts about this, it can steal our focus away from other things that we appreciate. We could miss noticing how funny our friend is because we're busy counting how many times they say 'like', or overlook the fact that they travelled three hours to come and see us, just because we're preoccupied with our annoyed thoughts of how much they talk about their kids.

In Chapter 5, *Without your presence, no connection*, we described how you can try to distinguish between thought problems and actual problems. Sometimes it helps to ask yourself: 'If I had *thought* less about this thing, would the problem have diminished?' If the answer is yes, you can try to focus a little less on your thoughts (even though they'll probably still pop up). In Chapter 6, *Entering your friend's world*, we also introduced the prism exercise, as a method of seeing more and new sides of a person. Together, these exercises can help us spend less energy on things that we don't want to, or cannot, change, and more energy on what makes us want to maintain and nurture the relationship.

Forgiveness brings freedom

If we've been hurt by a friend and if the wound hasn't healed, it can be hard to continue the friendship. If we haven't told our friend that we feel hurt, a good first step is to do just that. This gives our friend a chance to see our perspective and repair the damage. But what do we do if the wound remains unhealed?

When we feel that we've been hurt, offended or violated, it's not uncommon that we punish the other person in various, subtle ways. For instance, we can take revenge by withholding information, making snappy comments, or speaking badly of our friend in their absence. What does this result in? There's an old proverb that says: 'Holding a grudge is like drinking poison and hoping that the other person will die' – *we* ourselves are essentially the ones who suffer.

Researchers (for example Michael McCullough, psychologist and professor at the University of Miami) have found a connection between forgiveness and decreased levels of stress and anxiety. When we are able to forgive, we seem to experience increased feelings of control, relaxation and joy. In order to forgive someone, it's not necessary to diminish what they've done. The purpose is rather to free yourself, and spit out the toxic gum instead of continuing to chew it. Furthermore, forgiving someone doesn't mean that we have to let them back into our lives. However, if the relationship is important, forgiveness can help us to give them a new chance. The following exercise can help you initiate the process of forgiveness.

Reflection exercise: Forgive and be free

Purpose: Letting go of an injustice
Time required: 5–15 minutes
Method: Writing

This exercise is meant to plant a seed of forgiveness. It may help you to fully forgive a friend, but that doesn't necessarily have to be the goal. Instead, try to see this exercise as a way of opening up to new perspectives of your friend and of what happened.

1. *Get in touch with your wound.*

   Think about a situation where you felt hurt by a friend. Really try to envision the situation and allow all the feelings that arise. Try to stay with your feelings for a while – as long as you need – before moving on.

2. *Switch perspectives.*

   Now think about if there have been any situations when you yourself have acted in a similar way as your friend did in that situation. If you find such an example, write down the reasons why you acted as you did. Ask yourself which *need(s)* you were trying to accommodate.

3. *Write down three possible explanations of your friend's behaviour.*

   Now imagine your friend in this situation again. What could be the underlying reasons as to why they acted as they did? Write down at least three possible reasons. For example: 'They weren't feeling well', 'They were afraid of what others would think', 'They needed to express their frustration', 'They underestimated the risk of hurting me.'

4. *Write down what you could learn from this experience.*

   Upon contemplating what happened, is there anything that this experience has taught you? Perhaps you won't find the answer right away – give it some time.

5. *Ask yourself how ready you are to forgive.*

   On a scale from 0–10, how *good* would it be for you to let go of the injustice and forgive your friend? Using the same scale, how *ready* do you feel to do so?

6. *Write a letter.*

   Try writing a letter to the friend who hurt you. You never have to actually send it, but the point is to explore how it could feel to forgive this person, and how ready you are to do so. Include the following things in your letter:

   a) How you were hurt.

b) How you wish your friend would have acted instead.

c) That you forgive (or contemplate forgiving) your friend.

Forgiving someone is a process that can take time. When you do this exercise, you may discover that you're really not ready to let go. Perhaps you feel that the wound would get deeper by continued contact with this person. Maybe you come to the conclusion that you're better off protecting yourself by ending the friendship?

Breaking up

We're used to romantic relationships ending and we know what it means to break up as a couple. But what does it mean to break up with a friend? When can it be justified, and how is it done?

When friendships end, it's usually either just by fizzling out, or as a result of a conflict that we for some reason don't want to, or cannot, solve. However, friendships can also end because of a conscious decision. This should probably be used as a last resort, but it can be a kinder approach than to just avoid and ignore each other. When we try to punish a friend by, for example, making ourselves inaccessible, we can deepen the wound and cause bitterness for both ourselves and the other person. Therefore, it can be a gift to you both to take the bull by the horns and break up.

Try to end the friendship in a constructive way, by using I-statements and being clear and concise about why you're breaking up and how you want to move forward from here on. 'I've enjoyed a lot of the time we've spent together, but since X happened, I've felt insecure and I feel like our friendship costs more than it's worth. I can't see any possibility of changing that, so I want to end our friendship. I don't want us to talk to each other anymore.' It can be good to think about what you want to say, especially if you think that you might lose your temper. Try to avoid making accusations and placing blame – that will only cause tension that wears at the both of you. If possible, express the gratitude you feel for what you've shared (provided that it's honest).

In summary

There will always be some friction in friendships. Some of it can be avoided by clarifying our unspoken expectations. But one of the main points of this chapter is that we can use the energy that comes from conflicts to strengthen our relationships. This is possible if we dare to stay connected to ourselves and embrace discomfort, while remaining connected to the other person. In order to do so, we have to decide to prioritise connection even if, in the moment, it would be easier to escape. We have to be responsive to each other's perspectives while also taking responsibility for our own experiences. Taking responsibility for our own experience means expressing our needs and perspectives without placing blame or demanding a certain change. If we are able to see both our own and our friend's feelings and needs, it's easier for us to find strategies that benefit us both. The energy in the conflict can then be released and the connection deepened. Sand turns into pearls.

POSTSCRIPT

A few years have passed since we started writing this book. We were curious and wanted to learn more about how one could deepen bonds of friendship. We also recognised that friendship is so important to our own and others' wellbeing that it deserves more recognition. Toward the end of our process – which has been coloured by the end of the COVID-19 pandemic – the importance of friendship in our lives has become even more clear. During the pandemic, many of us were less social and felt more lonely than ever before.

Whether or not our book contributes to elevating the status of friendship remains to be seen, but writing it has undoubtedly been a rewarding journey for *us*. During the course of our collaboration we have had to practise what we preach – for example, expressing our own perspectives while also being responsive to each other's perspectives. Above all, we have been able to really sink our teeth into many of the most exciting, practical life questions that we know of: *What are the most common obstacles to close connection? What is vulnerability? Is it possible to be vulnerable while also feeling strong and comfortable? What does it mean to be present and what is self-awareness?* We have twisted and turned different models, discussed them with friends and family, and tried to apply them in our own lives. What have we authors learned from this journey? Here below, we give our joint opinion of the main message of this book:

Friendship is not *only* about enjoyment in the moment. When we nurture and cherish our friendships we also build longer, healthier and happier lives. Thus, friendship is something we can prioritise with good conscience. We strengthen our friendship bonds through repeatedly sharing moments of connection – which we in this book have referred to as pearls. A prerequisite for connecting with others is that we are in touch with ourselves: *What do I feel, what do I need and what am I curious about?* In a similar way, we need to be responsive to what's happening in the other person: *What feelings, needs and desires do you have?* Once we are aware of this, we can follow what's alive in the moment. It can mean venturing into uncharted territory. We may need to take risks and sometimes have the courage to relinquish what we believe to be expected of us. By exposing ourselves emotionally, we contribute to a culture of friendship where vulnerability, openness and trust can grow and thrive. In such cultures, emotional intimacy and sincere bonds can flourish.

If you've read this far, you've probably invested several hours of your time in exploring how you can develop your friendships and deepen your relationships. At the beginning of Chapter 3 (the friendship map exercise), you got to map out the direction you wanted to move towards. Have you already taken a few concrete steps in that direction? Perhaps you've changed *who* you spend time with and made new acquaintances, deepened existing relationships, or withdrawn from someone with whom you no longer feel that the friendship is worthwhile. Perhaps this process has inspired you to explore new ways of spending time together? If you've read the book with a friend, how has it affected your relationship? In Chapter 4, you mapped out your social skills. If you're up for it, go back and redo the exercise. Has anything changed? Take a moment to think about which insights have been the most useful to you. If you were to express what you have gotten out of this expedition, what would you say?

Creating and deepening friendships is, of course, a life-long process. Our hope is that this book has helped (and will continue to help) you to clarify where you want to go and how you are going to get there. The journey has only just begun.

Thank you

A lot of people have contributed to the origin and realisation of this book. First of all, we would like to thank Andrew McAleer, publisher at Little, Brown, for quickly latching on to our idea of translating this book, which was originally published in Swedish. We also want to thank Malin Hedeboe, trusted and loved sister of Frida, who implemented the English translation – we were highly impressed by how swiftly you transformed our text so that it now can reach a much broader audience. And Jess Haynie-Lavelle, a dear friend who has also proven to be a skilled editor – thank you for being so generous with your time and for slimming and polishing the text, making it even more appealing.

We would also like to thank our friends and family for valuable input about the book's content, as well as for invaluable psychological and practical support. A particularly warm thank you to Ragnar Bern, whose professional and linguistic ingenuity, tireless commitment and heroic efforts have benefited all three authors (not just Frida). A special thank you to Elin Gustavsson, for sharing your profound knowledge about NVC and of relationships in general, and for your suggestions about the layout of the book. And thank you to all those who have reassured us along the way that we're not completely off base – especially Björn Lannö, Anders Bern, Anders Eriksson, Erik Mägi, Robin Frostensson, Liria Ortiz, Heidi and Ray Fannon and our parents and siblings.

Hats off to all who have contributed, and continue to contribute, to express the ancient wisdom of how relationships deepen and strengthen. Mavis Tsai and Jonathan Kanter – when we realised that this book would be based on your simple but powerful models, a crucial piece of the puzzle fell into place. Thanks to all the grassroots, for example, the Authentic Relating and Burning Man movements, who passionately explore new methods of deepening connections. Also, thank you to all the participants in our courses – at Fridhems Community College, at the Friendship Lab, and at our unofficial Authentic Relating evenings. Hopefully, you've had as much fun as we have (even though you've sometimes had to be our guinea pigs).

Thanks to everyone who has facilitated our writing process. Thank you dear Kurt and Gertrud for all the times you've welcomed us and given us rides to your paradise in Djuvanäs! And thank you, dear Matilda and Rolf for all the blueberry pies and feasts of freshly harvested greens that you've served us in your peaceful Petikträsk! Thank you to all our generous and permissive bosses, who without the slightest squeak granted us time off work so that we've been able to write this book every Wednesday for several years!

Last but not least, we naturally want to thank our dear friends – you've taught us more about the importance of friendship than we could have ever learned through reading. In our circle of friends, we authors include each other. Such an endless number of long chat-conversations, video calls and writing retreats that we've devoted to this: our joint baby. How much we've evolved and learned from each other, both subject-wise and about the art of writing. Together, we've twisted and turned pretty much every word of this book – and the compromises haven't always been painless. Yet even during the most intense final phase, we've been tolerant with, and have sometimes even benefited from, each other's peculiarities: Pär's square research mind, Frida's wild impulses, and Daniel's pompous wordings. May our friendship continue to flourish.

References

Archie, E. A., Tung, J., Clark, M., Altmann, J., & Alberts, S. C. (2014), 'Social affiliation matters: both same-sex and opposite-sex relationships predict survival in wild female baboons', *Proceedings of the Royal Society B: Biological Sciences*, 281(1793), 20141261.

Aron A., et. al (1997), 'The experimental generation of interpersonal closeness: a procedure and some preliminary findings', *Personality and Social Psychology Bulletin*, Vol. 23, issue 4.

Aron, A., Aron E. N., & Smollan, D. (1992), 'Inclusion of other in the self scale and the structure of interpersonal closeness', *Journal of Personality and Social Psychology*, 63, 596–612.

Aron, A., Melinat, E., Aron, E. N., Vallone, R. D., & Bator, R. J. (1997), 'The experimental generation of interpersonal closeness: A procedure and some preliminary findings', *Personality and Social Psychology Bulletin*, 23(4), 363–377.

Aronson, E. (2004), *The Social Animal*, Ninth edition, Worth Publishers.

Aronson, E., & Mills, J. (1959), 'The effect of severity of initiation on liking for a group', *Journal of Abnormal and Social Psychology*, 59, 177–181.

Aronson, E., & Worchel, P. (1966), 'Similarity versus liking as determinants of interpersonal attractiveness', *Psychonomic Science*, 5(4), 157–158.

Ashton, M. C., Paunonen, S. V., Helmes, E., & Jackson, D. N. (1998), 'Kin altruism, reciprocal altruism, and the Big Five personality factors', *Evolution and Human Behavior*, 19, 243–255.

Baron, A. R., Byrne, D., Suls, J. (1989), *Exploring Social Psychology*, Third edition, Allyn and Bacon.

Bornstein, R. F., Leone, D. R., & Galley, D. J. (1987), 'The generalizability of subliminal mere exposure effects: Influence of stimuli perceived without awareness on social behavior', *Journal of Personality and Social Psychology*, 53(6), 1070.

Batool, S., & Malik, N. I. (2010), 'Role of attitude similarity and proximity in interpersonal attraction among friends (C 310)', *International Journal of Innovation, Management and Technology*, 1(2), 142.

Bayer, B., & Cunov, D. (n.d.), 'The authentic relating games night handbook', downloaded 31 March 2021, from http://online.anyflip.com/afbu/sfet/mobile/index.html#p=1

Bennich, A. (2019), *Att vinna över ensamheten*, Norstedts Förlag.

Berkman, L. F. et al. (2004), 'Social integration and mortality: A prospective study of French employees of Electricity of France–Gas of France: The GAZEL cohort', *American Journal of Epidemiology*, Volume 159, Issue 2, 15 January 2004, 167–174.

Boothby, E. J., Cooney, G., Sandstrom, G. M., & Clark, M. S. (2018), 'The liking gap in conversations: Do people like us more than we think?', *Psychological Science*, 29(11), 1742–1756.

Bornstein, R. F. (1989), 'Exposure and affect: overview and meta-analysis of research, 1968–1987', *Psychological Bulletin*, 106(2), 265.

Boye, K. (2014), *Gömda land*, Albert Bonniers Förlag.

Breit, S. et al. (2018), 'Vagus Nerve as Modulator of the Brain–Gut Axis in Psychiatric and Inflammatory Disorders', *Front Psychiatry*, 9:44.

Broberg, A., Granqvist, P., Ivarsson, T., & Risholm Mothander, P. (2006), *Anknytningsteori: Betydelsen av nära känslomässiga relationer*, Natur och Kultur, Stockholm.

Brockner, J., & Swap, W. C. (1976), 'Effects of repeated exposure and attitudinal similarity on self-disclosure and interpersonal attraction', *Journal of Personality and Social Psychology*, 33(5), 531–540.

Brown, B. (2015), *Mod att vara sårbar: i dina relationer, i ditt föräldraskap, i ditt arbete*, Libris.

Brown, B. (2016), *Våga vara operfekt*, Libris.

Byrne, D. (1969), 'Attitudes and attraction', *Advances in Experimental Psychology*, Vol 4.

Cacioppo, J. T., Hawkley, L. C., & Thisted, R. A. (2010), 'Perceived social isolation makes me sad: 5-year cross-lagged analyses of loneliness and depressive symptomatology in the Chicago Health, Aging, and Social Relations Study', *Psychology and Aging*, 25(2), 453.

Canary, D. J., Stafford, L., Hause, K. S., & Wallace, L. A. (1993), 'An inductive analysis of relational maintenance strategies: Comparisons among lovers, relatives, friends, and others', *Communication Research Reports*, 10(1), 3–14.

Canevello, A., & Crocker, J. (2010), 'Creating good relationships: responsiveness, relationship quality, and interpersonal goals', *Journal of Personality and Social Psychology*, *99*(1), 78.

Chapman, G. (1992), *The Five Love Languages: How to Express Heartfelt Commitment to Your Mate*, Northfield Press.

Christakis, N. A., & Fowler, J. H. (2009), *Connected: The Surprising Power of Our Social Networks and How They Shape Our Lives*, Little, Brown.

Cole, S. W. et al. (2007), 'Social regulation of gene expression in human leukocytes', *Genomic Biology*, *8*:R189.

Cole, S. W. (2009), 'Social regulation of human gene expression', *Current Directions in Psychological Science*, *18*(3),132–137.

Collins, N. L., & Miller, L. C. (1994), 'Self-disclosure and liking: a meta-analytic review', *Psychological Bulletin*, *116*(3), 457.

Csikszentmihalyi, M., & Hunter, J. (2014), 'Happiness in everyday life: The uses of experience sampling', in *Flow and the Foundations of Positive Psychology* (pp. 89–101), Springer, Dordrecht.

Deci, E., La Guardia, J. G., Moller, A. C., Scheiner, M. J., & Ryan, R. M. (2006), 'On the benefits of giving as well as receiving autonomy support: Mutuality in close friendships', *Personality and Social Psychology Bulletin*, 32.

Denworth, L. (2020), *Friendship: The Evolution, Biology, and Extraordinary Power of Life's Fundamental Bond*, WW Norton & Company.

Diamond, L. M., Fagundes, C. P., & Butterworth, M. R. (2012), 'Attachment style, vagal tone, and empathy during mother–adolescent interactions', *Journal of Research on Adolescence*, *22*(1), 165–184.

Diener, E., & Seligman, M. E. (2002), 'Very happy people', *Psychological Science*, *13*(1), 81–84.

Digges, J. (2020), *Conflict = Energy: The Transformative Practice of Authentic Relating*, ART International.

Duhigg, C. (2016), 'What Google learned from its quest to build the perfect team', *The New York Times Magazine*, *26*, 2016.

Ebbesen, E. B., Kjos, G. L., & Konečni, V. J. (1976), 'Spatial ecology: Its effects on the choice of friends and enemies', *Journal of Experimental Social Psychology*, *12*(6), 505–518.

Epley, N., & Schroeder, J. (2014), 'Mistakenly seeking solitude', *Journal of Experimental Psychology: General*, *143*(5), 1980.

Faustino, A. I., Tacão-Monteiro, A., & Oliveira, R. F. (2017), 'Mechanisms of social buffering of fear in zebrafish', *Scientific reports, 7*(1), 1–10.

Feeney, B. C., & Collins, N. L. (2003), 'Motivations for caregiving in adult intimate relationships: Influences on caregiving behavior and relationship functioning', *Personality and Social Psychology Bulletin, 29*(8), 950–968.

Fehr, B. (1996), *Friendship Processes* (Vol. 12), Sage.

Fowler, J. H., & Christakis, N. A. (2008), 'Dynamic spread of happiness in a large social network: longitudinal analysis over 20 years in the Framingham Heart Study', *The BMJ, 337.*

Fowler, J. H., & Christakis, N. A. (2010), 'Cooperative behavior cascades in human social networks', *Proceedings of the National Academy of Sciences, 107*(12), 5334–5338.

Frame, S. (2017, October 18), 'Julianne Holt-Lunstad probes loneliness, social connections', *American Psychological Association.* http://www.apa.org/members/content/holt-lunstad-loneliness-social-connections

Frederickson, J. (2017), *The Lies We Tell Ourselves: How to Face the Truth, Accept Yourself, and Create a Better Life*, Seven Leaves Press.

Fredrickson, B. L. (2001), 'The role of positive emotions in positive psychology: The broaden-and-build theory of positive emotions', *American Psychologist, 56*(3), 218.

Fredrickson, B. L. (2004), 'The broaden-and-build theory of positive emotions', *Philosophical Transactions of the Royal Society of London. Series B: Biological Sciences, 359*(1449), 1367–1377.

Fredrickson, B. L. (2013), *Love 2.0: Finding Happiness and Health in Moments of Connection*, Penguin.

Fredrickson, B. L., & Branigan, C. (2005), 'Positive emotions broaden the scope of attention and thought-action repertoires', *Cognition & Emotion, 19*(3), 313–332.

Gable, S. L., Gonzaga, G. C., & Strachman, A. (2006), 'Will you be there for me when things go right? Supportive responses to positive event disclosures', *Journal of Personality and Social Psychology, 91*(5), 904.

Gable, S. L. (2006), 'Approach and avoidance social motives and goals', *Journal of Personality, 74*(1), 175–222.

Gamer, M. et al (2010), 'Different amygdala subregions mediate valence-related and attentional effects of oxytocin in humans', *Proceedings of the National Academy of Sciences (USA) 107*(20), 9400–9405.

Gleason, M. E., Iida, M., Bolger, N., & Shrout, P. E. (2003), 'Daily supportive equity in close relationships', *Personality and Social Psychology Bulletin, 29*(8), 1036–1045.

Granovetter, M. S. (1973), 'The strength of weak ties', *American Journal of Sociology*, *78*(6), 1360–1380.

Grant, A. M. (2016), 'More evidence that learning economics makes you selfish', *Evonomics* *https://evonomics. com/more-evidence-that-learning -economics-makes-you-selfish*.

Hall, J. A. (2019), 'How many hours does it take to make a friend?', *Journal of Social and Personal Relationships*, *36*(4), 1278–1296.

Harrison, A. A. (1977), 'Mere exposure', in *Advances in Experimental Social Psychology* (Vol. 10, pp. 39–83), Academic Press.

Hassan, C. A. (2019), 'Feeling close to someone: The neural correlates of social connection', Bachelor Degree Project in Cognitive Neuroscience, University of Skövde.

Haworth, K., Kanter, J. W., Tsai, M., Kuczynski, A. M., Rae, J. R., & Kohlenberg, R. J. (2015), 'Reinforcement matters: A preliminary, laboratory-based component-process analysis of Functional Analytic Psychotherapy's model of social connection', *Journal of Contextual Behavioral Science*, *4*(4), 281–291.

Hayes, S. C., Sanford, B. T. (2014), 'Cooperation came first: evolution and human cognition', *Journal of the Experimental Analysis of Behavior*, *101*, 112–129.

Heaphy, E. D., & Dutton, J. E. (2008), 'Positive social interactions and the human body at work: Linking organizations and physiology', *Academy of Management Review*, *33*(1), 137–162.

Heider, F. (1958), *The Psychology of Interpersonal Relations*, New York: Wiley.

Heinrich, L. M., & Gullone, E. (2006), 'The clinical significance of loneliness: A literature review', *Clinical Psychology Review*, *26*(6), 695–718.

Hermes, G. L., Delgado, B., Tretiakova, M., Cavigelli, S. A., Krausz, T., Conzen, S. D., & McClintock, M. K. (2009), 'Social isolation dysregulates endocrine and behavioral stress while increasing malignant burden of spontaneous mammary tumors', *Proceedings of the National Academy of Sciences*, *106*(52), 22393–22398.

Holman, G., Kanter, J. W., Tsai, M., & Kohlenberg, R. (2017), *Functional Analytic Psychotherapy Made Simple: A Practical Guide to Therapeutic Relationships*, New Harbinger Publications.

Holt-Lunstad, J., & Smith, T. B. (2012), 'Social relationships and mortality', *Social and Personality Psychology Compass*, *6*(1), 41–53.

Holt-Lunstad, J., Robles, T. F., & Sbarra, D. A. (2017), 'Advancing social connection as a public health priority in the United States', *American Psychologist*, *72*(6), 517.

Holt-Lunstad, J., Smith, T. B., & Layton, J. B. (2010), 'Social relationships and mortality risk: A meta-analytic review', *PLoS Medicine*, *7*(7), e1000316.

Holt-Lunstad, J., Smith, T. B., Baker, M., Harris, T., & Stephenson, D. (2015), 'Loneliness and social isolation as risk factors for mortality: a meta-analytic review', *Perspectives on Psychological Science*, 10(2), 227–237.

Holt-Lunstad, J., Uchino, B. N., Smith, T. W., & Hicks, A. (2007), 'On the importance of relationship quality: The impact of ambivalence in friendships on cardiovascular functioning', *Annals of Behavioral Medicine*, 33(3), 278–290.

House, J. S., Landis, K. R., & Umberson, D. (1988), 'Social relationships and health', *Science*, New Series, 241(4865).

Howitt, D., Billig, M., Cramer, D., Edwards D., Kniveton, B., Potter, J., & Radley, A. (1989), *Social Psychology, Conflicts and Continuities*, Open University Press.

Jecker, J., & Landy, D. (1969), 'Liking a person as a function of doing him a favour', *Human Relations*, 22(4), 371–378.

Kahneman, D., Krueger, A. B., Schkade, D. A., Schwarz, N., & Stone, A. A. (2004), 'A survey method for characterizing daily life experience: The day reconstruction method', *Science*, 306(5702), 1776–1780.

Kanter, J. W., Kuczynski, A. M., Manbeck, K. E., Corey, M. D., & Wallace, E. C. (2020), 'An integrative contextual behavioral model of intimate relations', *Journal of Contextual Behavioral Science*.

Kanter, J.W., Kuczynski A.M., Tsai, M., & Kohlenberg, R. J. (2018), 'A brief contextual behavioral intervention to improve relationships: A randomized trial', *Journal of Contextual Behavioral Science*.

Kirsch, P. et al (2005), 'Oxytocin modulates neural circuitry for social cognition and fear in humans', *Journal of Neuroscience*, 25(49), 11489–11493.

Kok, B. E. (2012), *Testing the Socio-Autonomic Spiral Model of Social Connection and Health* (Doctoral dissertation, The University of North Carolina at Chapel Hill).

Kok, B. E., & Fredrickson, B. L. (2010), 'Upward spirals of the heart: autonomic flexibility, as indexed by vagal tone, reciprocally and prospectively predicts positive emotions and social connectedness', *Biological Psychology*, 85, 432–436.

Kok, B. E., Coffey, K. A., Cohn, M. A., Catalino, L. I., Vacharkulksemsuk, T., Algoe, S. B., . . . & Fredrickson, B. L. (2013), 'How positive emotions build physical health: Perceived positive social connections account for the upward spiral between positive emotions and vagal tone', *Psychological Science*, 24(7), 1123–1132.

Kumar, A., & Epley, N. (2018), 'Undervaluing gratitude: Expressers misunderstand the consequences of showing appreciation', *Psychological Science*, 29(9), 1423–1435.

Laurenceau, J. P., Barrett, L. F., & Pietromonaco, P. R. (1998), 'Intimacy as an interpersonal process: The importance of self-disclosure, partner disclosure, and perceived partner responsiveness in interpersonal exchanges', *Journal of Personality and Social Psychology*, 74(5), 1238.

Laurenceau, J. P., Barrett, L. F., & Rovine, M. J. (2005), 'The interpersonal process model of intimacy in marriage: a daily-diary and multilevel modeling approach', *Journal of Family Psychology*, 19(2), 314.

Laurenceau, J. P., Rivera, L. M., Schaffer, A. R., & Pietromonaco, P. R. (2004), 'Intimacy as an interpersonal process: Current status and future directions', *Handbook of Closeness and Intimacy*, 61–78.

Leung, P., Orrell, M., & Orgeta, V. (2015), 'Social support group interventions in people with dementia and mild cognitive impairment: a systematic review of the literature', *International Journal of Geriatric Psychiatry*, 30(1), 1–9.

Levitt, M. J. (1980), 'Contingent feedback, familiarization, and infant affect: How a stranger becomes a friend', *Developmental Psychology*, 16(5), 425.

Lippert, T., & Prager, K. J. (2001), 'Daily experiences of intimacy: A study of couples', *Personal Relationships*, 8(3), 283–298.

Livheim, F., Ek, D., & Hedensjö, B. (2017), *Tid att leva – ett tioveckorsprogram för stresshantering med ACT och Medveten närvaro*, Natur & Kultur.

Manbeck, K. E., Kanter, J. W., Kuczynski, A. M., Maitland, D. W., & Corey, M. (2020), 'Fear-of-intimacy in the interpersonal process model: An investigation in two parts', *Journal of Social and Personal Relationships*, 37(4), 1317–1339

May, J. L., & Hamilton, P. A. (1980), 'Effects of musically evoked affect on women's interpersonal attraction toward and perceptual judgments of physical attractiveness of men', *Motivation and Emotion*, 4(3), 217–228.

McCullough, M. E., Bellah, C. G., Kilpatrick, S. D., & Johnson, J. L. (2001), 'Vengefulness: Relationships with forgiveness, rumination, well-being, and the Big Five', *Personality and Social Psychology Bulletin*, 27, 601–610.

McCullough, M. E., Rachal, K. C., Sandage, S. J., Worthington, E. L., Brown, S. W., & Hight, T. L. (1998), 'Interpersonal forgiving in close relationships: II. Theoretical elaboration and measurement', *Journal of Personality and Social Psychology*, 75, 1586–1603.

McCullough, M. E., Worthington, E. L., & Rachal, K. C. (1997), 'Interpersonal forgiving in close relationships', *Journal of Personality and Social Psychology*, 73, 321–336.

McNiel, J. M., & Fleeson, W. (2006), 'The causal effects of extraversion on positive affect and neuroticism on negative affect: Manipulating state extraversion and state neuroticism in an experimental approach', *Journal of Research in Personality*, 40(5), 529–550.

Mogilner, C. (2010), 'The pursuit of happiness: Time, money, and social connection', *Psychological Science*, 21(9), 1348–1354.

Morelli, S. A., Torre, J. B., & Eisenberger, N. I. (2014), 'The neural bases of feeling understood and not understood', *Social Cognitive and Affective Neuroscience*, 9(12), 1890–1896.

Nelson K., Yang J., Maliken A., Kohlenberg, R., Tsai, M. (2013), 'Introduction to using structured evocative activities in functional analytic psychotherapy', *Cognitive and Behavioral Practice*, 23.

Ofman, D. (2001), *Core Qualities: A Gateway to Human Resources*, Schiedam: Scriptum.

Oswald, D. L., Clark, E. M., & Kelly, C. M. (2004), 'Friendship maintenance: An analysis of individual and dyad behaviors', *Journal of Social and Clinical Psychology*, 23(3), 413–441.

Padula, A. (2009), 'Kinesics', in S. Littlejohn, & K. Foss (Eds.), *Encyclopedia of Communication Theory* (pp. 582–584), Thousand Oaks, CA: Sage.

Kåver, A., & Nilsonne, Å. (2019), *Tillsammans*, Natur & Kultur.

Parkinson, B. (1996), 'Emotions are social', *British Journal of Psychology*, 87, 663–683.

Parlee, M. B. (1979), 'The friendship bond', *Psychology Today*, 13(4), 43–54.

Petrovic P. et al (2008), 'Oxytocin attenuates affective evaluations of conditioned faces and amygdala activity', *Journal of Neuroscience*, 28(26), 6607–6615.

Poorthuis, A. M., Thomaes, S., Denissen, J. J., van Aken, M. A., & de Castro, B. O. (2012), 'Prosocial tendencies predict friendship quality, but not for popular children', *Journal of Experimental Child Psychology*, 112(4), 378–388.

Priest, R. F., & Sawyer, J. (1967), 'Proximity and peership: Bases of balance in interpersonal attraction', *American Journal of Sociology*, 72(6), 633–649.

Rademacher, L., Schulte-Rüther, M., Hanewald, B., & Lammertz, S. (2015), 'Reward: from basic reinforcers to anticipation of social cues', *Social Behavior from Rodents to Humans*, 207–221.

Reis, H. T., Shaver, P., Duck, S., & Hay, D. F. (1988), 'Intimacy as an interpersonal process', *Handbook of Personal Relationships*.

Reis, H. T., Sheldon, K. M., Gable, S. L., Roscoe, J., & Ryan, R. M. (2000), 'Daily well-being: The role of autonomy, competence, and relatedness', *Personality and Social Psychology Bulletin*, 26(4), 419–435.

Roderik, J. S. G. & Guido, P. H. B. (2018), 'Breath of life: The respiratory vagal stimulation model of contemplative activity', *Frontiers in Human Neuroscience*, 12, 397.

Rosenberg, M. B. (2007), *Nonviolent Communication: ett språk för livet*. Friare liv konsult.

Ross, L. (1977), 'The intuitive psychologist and his shortcomings: Distortions in the attribution process', in *Advances in Experimental Social Psychology* (Vol. 10, pp. 173–220), Academic Press.

Saegert, S., Swap, W., & Zajonc, R. B. (1973), 'Exposure, context, and interpersonal attraction', *Journal of Personality and Social Psychology, 25*(2), 234.

Schneiderman, I. et al. (2012), 'Oxytocin during the initial stages of romantic attachment: Relations to couples' interactive reciprocity', *Psychoneuroendocrinology, 37*(8), 1277–1285.

Seyfarth, R. M., & Cheney, D. L. (2012), 'The evolutionary origins of friendship', *Annual Review of Psychology, 63*, 153–177.

Sherif, M. (1956), 'Experiments in group conflict', *Scientific American, 195*, 53–58.

Siette, J., Cassidy, M., & Priebe, S. (2017), 'Effectiveness of befriending interventions: a systematic review and meta-analysis', *BMJ Open, 7*(4).

Silk, J. B. (2002), 'Using the "F"-word in primatology', *Behaviour, 139*(2), 421–446.

Silk, J. B., Alberts, S. C., & Altmann, J. (2003), 'Social bonds of female baboons enhance infant survival', *Science, 302*(5648), 1231–1234.

Silk, J. B., Alberts, S. C., & Altmann, J. (2006), 'Social relationships among adult female baboons (*Papio cynocephalus*) II. Variation in the quality and stability of social bonds', *Behavioral Ecology and Sociobiology, 61*(2), 197–204.

Silk, J. B., Altmann, J., & Alberts, S. C. (2006), 'Social relationships among adult female baboons (*Papio cynocephalus*) I. Variation in the strength of social bonds', *Behavioral Ecology and Sociobiology, 61*(2), 183–195.

Silk, J. B., Beehner, J. C., Bergman, T. J., Crockford, C., Engh, A. L., Moscovice, L. R., . . . & Cheney, D. L. (2009), 'The benefits of social capital: close social bonds among female baboons enhance offspring survival', *Proceedings of the Royal Society B: Biological Sciences, 276*(1670), 3099–3104.

Silk, J. B., Beehner, J. C., Bergman, T. J., Crockford, C., Engh, A. L., Moscovice, L. R., . . . & Cheney, D. L. (2010), 'Strong and consistent social bonds enhance the longevity of female baboons', *Current Biology, 20*(15), 1359–1361.

Sloan, E. K., Capitanio, J. P., Tarara, R. P., Mendoza, S. P., Mason, W. A., & Cole, S. W. (2007), 'Social stress enhances sympathetic innervation of primate lymph nodes: Mechanisms and implications for viral pathogenesis', *Journal of Neuroscience, 27*(33), 8857–8865.

Smith, K. J., Gavey, S., Riddell, N. E., Kontari, P., & Victor, C. (2020), 'The association between loneliness, social isolation and inflammation: A systematic review and meta-analysis', *Neuroscience & Biobehavioral Reviews*, *112*, 519–541.

Sofer, O. J. (2018), *Say What You Mean: A Mindful Approach to Nonviolent Communication*, Shambhala Publications.

Sommerlad, A., Sabia, S., Singh-Manoux, A., Lewis, G., & Livingston, G. (2019), 'Association of social contact with dementia and cognition: 28-year follow-up of the Whitehall II cohort study', *PLoS Medicine*, *16*(8), e1002862.

Srivastava, S., Tamir, M., McGonigal, K. M., John, O. P., & Gross, J. J. (2009), 'The social costs of emotional suppression: A prospective study of the transition to college', *Journal of Personality and Social Psychology*, *96*, 883–897.

Stone, D., & Heen, S. (2015), *Thanks for the Feedback: The Science and Art of Receiving Feedback Well (even when it is off base, unfair, poorly delivered, and frankly, you're not in the mood)*, Penguin.

Tangney, J., Fee, R., Reinsmith, C., Boone, A.L., & Lee, N. (1999, August), 'Assessing individual differences in the propensity to forgive', paper presented at the annual meeting of the American Psychological Association, Boston.

Thayer, J. F., Sternberg, E. (2006), 'Beyond heart rate variability: Vagal regulation of allostatic systems', *Annals of the New York Academy of Sciences*, *1088*, 361–372.

Tsai, M., Kohlenberg, R. J., Kanter, J., Kohlenberg, B., Follette, W., & Callaghan, G. (2009), *A Guide to Functional Analytic Psychotherapy: Awareness, Courage, Love and Behaviorism*, New York: Springer.

Uchino, B. N. (2004), *Social Support and Physical Health: Understanding the Health Consequences of Relationships*, Yale University Press.

Uchino, B. N., Cawthon, R. M., Smith, T. W., Light, K. C., McKenzie, J., Carlisle, M., . . . & Bowen, K. (2012), 'Social relationships and health: Is feeling positive, negative, or both (ambivalent) about your social ties related to telomeres?', *Health Psychology*, *31*(6), 789.

Van Dam, H. A., van der Horst, F. G., Knoops, L., Ryckman, R. M., Crebolder, H. F., & van den Borne, B. H. (2005), 'Social support in diabetes: A systematic review of controlled intervention studies', *Patient Education and Counseling*, *59*(1), 1–12.

Van Kleef, G. A. (2010), 'The emerging view of emotion as social information', *Social and Personality Psychology Compass*, *4*(5), 331–343.

Venniro, M., Zhang, M., Caprioli, D., Hoots, J. K., Golden, S. A., Heins, C., . . . & Shaham, Y. (2018), 'Volitional social interaction prevents drug addiction in rat models', *Nature Neuroscience*, *21*(11), 1520–1529.

Wagner, U., Galli, L., Schott, B. H., Wold, A., van der Schalk, J., Manstead, A. S., . . . & Walter, H. (2015), 'Beautiful friendship: Social sharing of emotions improves subjective feelings and activates the neural reward circuitry', *Social Cognitive and Affective Neuroscience, 10*(6), 801–808.

Waldinger, R. (2015), 'What makes a good life? Lessons from the longest study on happiness', TedX videoklipp, www.ted.com

Ware, B. (2012), *The Top Five Regrets of the Dying: A Life Transformed by the Dearly Departing*, Hay House, Inc.

Watson, J. B. (1928), *Psychological Care of Infant and Child*, WW Norton & Company.

Wilson, K. G. (2014), *The ACT Matrix: A New Approach to Building Psychological Flexibility Across Settings and Populations*, New Harbinger Publications.

Zajonc, R. B. (2001), 'Mere exposure: A gateway to the subliminal', *Current Directions in Psychological Science, 10*(6), 224–228.

Zhao, X., & Epley, N. (2021), 'Kind words do not become tired words: Undervaluing the positive impact of frequent compliments', *Self and Identity, 20*(1), 25–46.

APPENDIX 1

Extra games and portable tools

Here, you will find extra games and portable tools. All but 'Verbalise your feelings' are done with two or more participants. We've divided them into the categories 'Playful and light-hearted' and 'Intimate and potentially challenging'.

Playful and light-hearted
1. *The lie-detector* – reveal if your friend is lying
2. *The dating game* – find out what your friend prefers, and is triggered by, on dates
3. *Search for similarities* – explore what you have in common and what makes you unique

Intimate and potentially challenging
4. *Speaker circle* – get a deeper insight into your friends' lives right now
5. *Checking in* – quickly becoming present together with friends, acquaintances, or colleagues
6. *I can relate* – share each other's emotional world
7. *Thirty-six questions* – create closeness using scientifically proven questions
8. *The hot seat* – ask brave questions and get to know each other on a more profound level

9. *Your story and my story* – become closer using questions about each other's childhood
10. *Verbalise your feelings* – become better at understanding and affirming your feelings

Playful and light-hearted

1. The lie-detector

Purpose: To get to know each other by playing with the theme true or false
Time required: 15–60 minutes
Method: Verbally with at least one friend

In this exercise, you get to test your ability to see through each other's lies. You also get to take part in stories from each other's lives that you may not have known about before. This can be a fun and light-hearted way of getting to know each other better.

Read the instructions and decide who will be person A before starting.

1. *Person A comes up with three statements about themself.*
   Two statements should be true and one false. They should all be things that the other person doesn't already know about you, so that it's not too easy to decide which is true and which is false. If it feels difficult to come up with three statements, you can choose something banal, like what you had for breakfast this morning. Other suggestions of subjects are: Events from primary school, old clothing items, embarrassing moments, previous jobs, things you've lied about, peculiarities of family members, etc.
2. *Person A shares their statements.*
   The goal is to make the other person believe that all three statements are true.
3. *The other person (or the other people) 'guess the lie'.*
   In turn, the other participants guess which statement they believe to be false, preferably motivating their answers.

4. *Person A reveals which statement is false.*
5. *Switch roles.*

2. The dating game

Purpose: To get to know each other's preferences when it comes to dating

Time required: 30–90 minutes

Method: Verbally with at least one friend, and writing

For this game you need paper, pens and preferably a pair of scissors. The game is a fun way of getting to know each other's preconceptions, sensitivities and triggers when it comes to dating and romantic partners. Everyone can do this exercise, even if they already have a partner.

1. *Write down characteristics and attributes.*

   The game starts with all the participants writing down different characteristics and attributes of people that the participants will pretend to go on a date with. Write *one* thing on each piece of paper, for example: 'Has an IQ of 140', 'Is at least 6-ft tall', 'Has dated your sibling', 'Is allergic to dogs', 'Collects stamps', 'Can't cook', 'Votes for *X political party*', etc. Let your imagination run wild! Every participant can write as many pieces of paper as they want, but a rule of thumb is that each person writes at least five notes.

2. *Collect the notes.*

   Fold all the notes and put them in a pile (preferably in a bowl or hat).

3. *Take one note and decide.*

   The participants then take turns taking a note from the pile. The note you pick describes your date. You read what it says aloud to the others and then decide how you want to move forward. If you want to go on a second date with this fictional person, you save your note for the next round. If you want to stop dating the person, you throw away the note (it is now out of the game) and start over in the next round. Regardless of what you choose, defend your answer.

4. *Take new notes.*

   When everyone has finished the first round it's time to draw new notes. If you still have a note (or several) from the previous round(s), you read it/them aloud to the others again. The new note you've picked is added to the overall description of your date (they may be 6-ft tall, collect stamps, and vote for the Labour party). Again, you decide if you want to keep dating this person, or if you want to end it and start over in the next round.

5. *Continue until you have gone through all the notes.*

3. Search for similarities

Purpose: To create connection through exploring what you have in common and what makes you unique
Time required: 15–45 minutes
Method: Verbally with at least one friend

Searching for similarities can be a powerful way of creating a sense of belonging in a group. The game can be suitable during a train ride, around a dinner table, or at a party. It can be played in a context where all the people don't know each other, or together with old friends – you may discover both similarities and differences that you weren't previously aware of.

1. *Search for similarities.*

   Find different things that you have in common by talking to each other. A rule of thumb is to find as many similarities as there are participants in the game, so if you're five people playing, try to find five things that you all have in common. Try to avoid similarities that are too simple and obvious, for instance that you're human, live in the same country, and so on. Instead, try to find similarities that are more personally relevant, for example: 'We all have parents that are divorced',

'We've all at some point been thrown out of a bar', 'We've all failed our driving test', 'We've all called in sick to work even though we weren't actually sick', etc.

2. *Search for differences.*

Find one thing that's unique to each person by talking to each other. This can be an opportunity to share things about yourself that the others weren't aware of, for example: 'I have obsessive compulsive disorder' or 'I've won the karate state championship.'

Intimate and potentially challenging

4. Speaker circle

Purpose: To obtain a more profound connection through talking about important things in your life (and listening to the others' stories)
Time required: 10–120 minutes
Method: Verbally with at least one friend

The purpose of a speaker circle (or 'sharing', as it's sometimes referred to) is to gain insight into what's important in the others' lives, and to be listened to. During the round, each person gets a chance to share what they want, without having to compete to get the others' attention. A good starting point is that everyone gets to share something from the theme: 'What is most present in me right now?' It could be something that feels significant in your life at the moment, your emotional state then and there, or how it feels to be in the room with the group. Make sure you're in a place where you can talk and listen without being interrupted.

1. *Set the frame.*

Decide on how long each person will have to talk (we suggest 2–20 minutes per person) and set a timer. Also make sure you all agree that everything that is said in the circle never leaves the room.

2. *Centre yourselves.*

    Sit in a way that allows you all to see and hear each other well, for example in a circle. Centre yourselves in the present moment by taking a few minutes to focus on your body and your breathing. Then, ask all the participants to let go of their plans of what they are going to talk about, and trust that something will pop up when it's their turn. Remind everyone to listen attentively, without judging or commenting, to create a safe and free space for the person who's speaking.

3. *One person begins to speak. The rest listen.*

    The time period is for the person who's talking, and they themself decide what to talk about. It can be good to remind the person that their task *isn't* to entertain or in other ways try to please the listeners, but to focus on what's present inside themself and what they want to share in that moment. Slowing down and allowing pauses can often help. Set a timer. When it rings, the speaker rounds off and ends by letting the others know he/she is finished (for example by saying 'Thank you').

4. *The next person takes over.*

    Choose if you want to take turns in a specific order or if you want to do it 'popcorn-style', where anyone can jump in when the previous speaker is done talking.

5. *End the round.*

    When everyone has had their turn, you can end the round together by, for example, all being quiet for a few minutes, or by thanking each other in some other way that feels natural to you.

Version II: two rounds. Another option, that's a little more intimate, is doing two or more rounds. In the second round you can share how you were affected by what someone said during the first round. Perhaps you were moved by something? Maybe you could relate to something one of the other participants shared? Let everyone have a turn.

5. Checking in

Purpose: Creating connection through checking in and touching base about where you are in your lives, here and now
Time required: 3–20 minutes
Method: Verbally with at least one friend

Checking in is a shorter and simpler version of the speaker circle. It's a simple and powerful tool that can be used in several different contexts, to unite a group and give everyone an opportunity to talk and to see each other. It can be used at a party, a dinner or at other events, so that everyone can get acquainted and touch base about how each person is doing. 'Checking in' means briefly saying how you are here and now, through, for example, answering one or some of the following questions. 'How has my day been so far?', 'What's important to me in my life right now?' or 'How am I doing, here and now?' If it's an event where not everyone knows each other, another version can be that each person shares how they know the host/hostess. Checking in can also be a good routine within a workplace environment – when you come to work or as a way to start a meeting.

1. *Initiate and explain.*
   Suggest doing a round of checking in by explaining what it implies and making sure that everyone is up for it. Agree on which question to answer, and decide how long each person will get to talk. If you want, you can use a timer that rings after 1–3 minutes, to help you divide the time equally.

2. *Start the round.*
   The person who starts checking in does so by answering the question(s) you have chosen. Those who listen don't comment on anything, but just sit quietly and listen. The speaker indicates clearly when they're finished (for example by saying 'Thank you'), and yields the floor to the next person. Continue through the round, letting everyone speak in turn.

Version II: Checking out. Just as it can be a good idea to start a weekly meeting at work with a brief session of checking in, it can also be valuable to end a meeting by checking out. This is especially beneficial if the participants of the meeting have feelings and thoughts that they need to vent. Or if there is a need for a collective review of what was decided during the meeting.

6. I can relate [17]

Purpose: To stimulate empathy and connection
Time required: 15–30 minutes
Method: Verbally with at least one friend

In this exercise, you will get to talk about emotions you've experienced in different situations in your life. It can be a good way to take part in each other's emotional worlds and obtain a deeper understanding of one another. Read the instructions and decide who will start as person A and who will start as person B before you begin.

1. *Person A chooses three emotions.*

   Person A, choose three emotions that you've felt at some point during your life. You may have felt them all at once or at different times. Regardless, name the emotions without putting them into context.

2. *Person B talks about the emotions.*

   Person B, talk about when you have experienced these same emotions in your own life. Unlike person A, you talk about the background stories of when you felt these emotions. What was the situation or context? You don't necessarily have to have experienced them all at the same time, you can just as well talk about three different situations if you want.

3. *Person A shares what they've learned.*

   Person A, now share what you feel that you've learned from hearing person B talk about these emotions. Also share if and how you were affected by what B said, and what you could (and/or could not) relate to.

4. *Switch roles.*

---

17 This exercise is adapted from *The Authentic Relating Games Manual* and was invented by Zachary Robison of Authentic Houston.

7. Thirty-six questions

Purpose: To establish a connection by taking turns to ask and answer increasingly personal questions
Time required: 3–45 minutes
Method: Verbally with at least one friend

These questions are from a study conducted at the State University of New York in 1997. The researchers wanted to see if it was possible to get strangers to feel closer to each other by letting them ask and answer increasingly personal questions during a time period of 45 minutes. It was – to a surprisingly high degree. Some of the participants felt as close, or closer, to the other person than to anyone else in their lives. These questions are often referred to as the 'thirty-six questions that lead to love'. They are listed here below, divided into three levels, where the degree of intimacy increases with each level. The idea is that each question should be answered by you both before moving on to the next one.

Level 1

1. Given the choice of anyone in the world, whom would you want as a dinner guest?
2. Would you like to be famous? In what way?
3. Before making a telephone call, do you ever rehearse what you are going to say? Why?
4. What would constitute a 'perfect' day for you?
5. When did you last sing to yourself? To someone else?
6. If you were able to live to the age of ninety and retain either the mind or body of a thirty-year-old for the last sixty years of your life, which would you want?
7. Do you have a secret hunch about how you will die?
8. Name three things you and your partner appear to have in common.
9. For what in your life do you feel most grateful?
10. If you could change anything about the way you were raised, what would it be?

11. Take four minutes and tell your partner your life story in as much detail as possible.

12. If you could wake up tomorrow having gained any one quality or ability, what would it be?

Level 2

13. If a crystal ball could tell you the truth about yourself, your life, the future or anything else, what would you want to know?

14. Is there something that you've dreamed of doing for a long time? Why haven't you done it?

15. What is the greatest accomplishment of your life?

16. What do you value most in a friendship?

17. What is your most treasured memory?

18. What is your most terrible memory?

19. If you knew that in one year you would die suddenly, would you change anything about the way you are now living? Why?

20. What does friendship mean to you?

21. What roles do love and affection play in your life?

22. Alternate sharing something you consider a positive characteristic of your partner. Share a total of five items.

23. How close and warm is your family? Do you feel your childhood was happier than most other people's?

24. How do you feel about your relationship with your mother?

Level 3

25. Make three true 'we' statements each. For instance, 'We are both in this room feeling . . . '

26. Complete this sentence: 'I wish I had someone with whom I could share . . . '

27. If you were going to become a close friend with your game partner, please share what would be important for them to know.

28. Tell your partner what you like about them; be very honest this time, saying things that you might not say to someone you've just met.

29. Share with your partner an embarrassing moment in your life.

30. When did you last cry in front of another person? By yourself?

31. Tell your partner something that you like about them [already].

32. What, if anything, is too serious to be joked about?

33. If you were to die this evening with no opportunity to communicate with anyone, what would you most regret not having told someone? Why haven't you told them yet?

34. Your house, containing everything you own, catches fire. After saving your loved ones and pets, you have time to safely make a final dash to save any one item. What would it be? Why?

35. Of all the people in your family, whose death would you find most disturbing? Why?

36. Share a personal problem and ask your partner's advice on how they might handle it. Also, ask your partner to reflect back to you how you seem to be feeling about the problem you have chosen.

8. The hot seat[18]

Purpose: To stimulate curiosity, openness, and connection
Time required: 10–90 minutes
Method: Verbally with at least one friend

This exercise is about asking questions – that you're genuinely curious about – to a person sitting in the 'hot seat'. The person in the hot seat should sit in a place where all the others can see them, like a teacher in front of their class.

1. *Decide how long each person should sit in the hot seat.*
   A suitable time frame can be somewhere between 7 and 15 minutes. Use a timer to divide the time equally between the participants.

2. *Choose a person.*
   Choose who will start being person A and sit in the hot seat.

---

18 This exercise is originally from an organisation called Authentic World and is described in the book *Authentic Relating Games Manual*.

3. *Ask questions.*

The other participants may now start asking questions to person A. Those who want to pose a question raise their hand, and person A gives the floor by pointing. When asking questions, let your genuine curiosity guide you – what are you really interested in finding out? When you've asked your question and feel satisfied, you say 'Thank you' to give the next person the opportunity to ask a question.

4. *Person A answers the questions they want.*

The person in the hot seat (A) only answers the questions they want to answer. If A gets a question that they don't want to answer, they can ask for another one right away. When the time is up it can be a good idea to check with A how they feel, and if there might be some unresolved issue left lingering that they want to talk about. Thereafter, the next volunteer takes a seat in the hot seat.

Version II: Connection round after each set

An alternative version is that you finish each set with a round where all the participants get to answer the question: 'When did you feel the most connected to person A?' Perhaps there was a moment where A lit up a little extra or was particularly personal and open about their feelings? All the participants answer the question by finishing the phrase: 'I felt the most connected to you when you . . . '

Version III: The dead seat

The person in the hot seat imagines that they have died, and talks about their life and how they see it now from 'the other side'. The other participants ask questions in a similar way as in the previous rounds, but this time the questions regard the life that person A has already lived.

9. *Your story and my story*[19]

Purpose: To gain a deeper understanding of yourself and your friend by looking back at your childhood
Time required: 30–90 minutes
Method: Verbally with at least one friend

---

19 This exercise is from the book *Roots to Love*, Lemarc Thomas, 2021, www.lemarcthomas.com

This exercise is a type of interview that you can do with a friend. The idea is to stimulate a conversation about your childhoods, your relationships with your parents (or whoever raised you), and how they have affected you. The exercise can be done in two ways: a) Start by answering the questions in writing, and then share your answers with each other, or b) Let one person pose the questions to the other person and then switch roles. Whatever you choose, be sure to set aside enough time and that you're able to go through the exercise without being disturbed.

1. Where were you born and who took care of you?
2. Who was in your family? What did your parents (or those who raised you) do for a living?
3. What kind of environment did you grow up in? Describe the surroundings.
4. How would you describe yourself as a child? What kinds of thoughts and feelings did you use to have?
5. Which five words would you use to describe your parents (or those who raised you)? Use five words for each person.
6. Describe your relationship with your parents as a child. Start by sharing your earliest memories.
7. Which parent (or person who raised you) did you feel the closest to, and why?
8. Was there anything you experienced that your parents easily gave you? If so – what? For example: time, praise, money, practical help, comfort.
9. Did you feel like you had to be a certain way in order to get their love? If so – how?
10. What did you do when you were upset?
11. Was there anything you experienced that your parents had to struggle to give you? If so – what? For example: time, praise, money, practical help, comfort.
12. How do you think your experiences with your parents have affected you? How is it reflected in your life today?

13. Why do you think your parents acted as they did during your childhood?
14. What positive things have your upbringing contributed to your life today?

10. Verbalise your feelings

Purpose: To put words to your feelings, to make it easier to feel, express and be with them
Time required: 3–5 minutes
Method: Mentally

Painful and unpleasant emotions can often be experienced as even more uncomfortable when you try to get rid of them. They're like a persistent postman who wants to deliver a package to you. If you don't open the door when the postman rings the doorbell, he keeps coming back day after day to deliver your package. This exercise can help you put words to your painful feelings, and thereby make it easier for you to meet them. You can do this exercise after a difficult social situation, but you can also do it on the spur of the moment – when you're in the middle of something that feels difficult.

1. *Think about a difficult situation.*
   Choose a recent (or current) situation that was (or is) difficult for you in some way. Perhaps you felt uncomfortable, secluded, disconnected, scared, left out, sad or angry. Something didn't feel right. If it helps, close your eyes and try to make the memory as vivid as possible by going back and placing yourself in the situation.
2. *Focus and place a hand on your body.*
   How does it feel to think about this? Can you sense the feelings somewhere in your body? Do you feel that any particular area is activated, tense or perhaps dull? If you'd like, you can try placing your hand on the area where you experience the feeling the most clearly.

3.   *Try to put words to your feelings.*
     Now try to verbalise what you're feeling, aloud or in your own mind, for example: 'I feel sad', 'I feel angry', or 'I feel sad AND angry.' If you want, you can use the list of emotions here below.
4.   *Make room for the emotions.*
     Imagine that the hand you placed on your body invites the feelings in and clears more space for them inside of you. If you want, you can say something like: 'I'm giving my emotions as much space as they need' or 'It's OK for me to feel this way.'
5.   *Act lovingly.*
     What would be a loving way to meet yourself here and now? Could you give yourself that?

List of emotions

Seclusion	Sadness	Guilt	Irritation	Anxiety	Restlessness
Indifference	Disappointment	Shame	Anger	Panic	Nervousness
Emptiness	Grief	Disgust	Hatred	Jealousy	Concern
Depression	Aversion	Abhorrence	Rage	Envy	Fear
Love	Gratitude	Pride	Joy	Amazement	Surprise
Happiness	Curiosity	Interest	Frustration	Stress	Euphoria

APPENDIX 2

Websites, courses and other resources

- www.relationalmindfulness.online – online training in Relational Mindfulness® to deepen awareness and courage in relationships.
- www.livewithacl.org – Live with Awareness, Courage and Love, a non-profit organisation with meet ups all over the world.
- 29k.org – 29k is a free app where you, together with others, get to practise openness and vulnerability and other interpersonal skills, while working as a group on different themes, such as relationships, self-compassion, values and stress management.
- authenticrelating.co – Authentic Relating Training International, providing courses online and all over the world in authentic relating training.
- theconnectioninstitute.net – The Connection Institute, training facilitators and providing courses and events to deepen connection
- www.authrev.org – Authentic Revolution, providing online courses and training in authentic relating.
- www.circlinginstitute.com – The Circling Institute provides courses and training in the relational mindfulness method called 'Circling'.
- www.circleanywhere.com – Circle Anywhere provide training in Circling online.

- www.circlingeurope.com – Circling Europe provide training online and in Europe.
- *The Authentic Relating Games Night Handbook* – a booklet in English with lots of connection promoting games that can be downloaded from the internet free of charge or by donation.

Index